KEEPING IT REAL

IN THE REAL WORLD

Also by Becky De Oliveira:

Your Angel
What Shall I Dream About?

To order, call 1-800-765-6955.

Visit us at
www.reviewandherald.com
for information on other Review and Herald® products.

KEEPING IT REAL

IN THE REAL WORLD

BECKY DE OLIVEIRA

REVIEW AND HERALD® PUBLISHING ASSOCIATION
Since 1861 | www.reviewandherald.com

Published by Review and Herald® Publishing Association, Hagerstown, MD 21741-1119

Review and Herald® titles may be purchased in bulk for educational, business, fund-raising, or sales promotional use. For information, e-mail SpecialMarkets@reviewandherald.com.

The Review and Herald® Publishing Association publishes biblically based materials for spiritual, phys-ical, and mental growth and Christian discipleship.

The author assumes full responsibility for the accuracy of all facts and quotations as cited in this book.

This book was
Edited by Kalie Kelch
Copyedited by Judy Blodgett
Designed by Emily Harding
Cover art by istockphoto.com
Typeset: Bembo 11/13.5

PRINTED IN U.S.A.

15   14   13   12   11   5   4   3   2   1

Library of Congress Cataloging-in-Publication Data
De Oliveira, Becky.
   Keeping it real in the real world / Becky De Oliveira.
      p. cm. — (2012 young adult devotional)
   1. Young adults—Prayers and devotions. 2. Seventh-Day Adventists—Prayers and devotions. I. Title.
   BV4850.D46 2011
   242'.64—dc23
                                    2011016903

ISBN 978-0-8280-2502-7

DEDICATION

Mrs. Zbaraschuk,
this may not be at all what you had in mind when you tried to teach me
how to write, but all the same, it's for you.

Humanity i love you because you
are perpetually putting the secret of
life in your pants and forgetting
it's there and sitting down

e. e. cummings

CONTENTS

INTRODUCTION:
TWO CHAIRS

I TEACH PRIMARILY doctoral students, and the phrase "life happens"—or a variation—is one I hear often when students talk about the extent to which they've gotten sidetracked on writing their dissertations. The words are said with a shrug and generally without bitterness. It's a philosophical statement and one that pretty much sums everything up. This is what happens to us. *Life.* Nothing tends to turn out the way we planned or hoped, although that isn't always a bad thing. There is, of course, a famous saying that goes like this: "Life is what happens while you're busy making other plans."

Sometimes I realize, with a sudden shot of panic straight to the throat, that I live in Berrien Springs, Michigan, and I'm not at all sure how I *got* here. I mean, I know how I got here, but I don't know how I *got here,* if you see what I'm getting at. The last thing I really remember clearly was getting on a plane to England when I was 21 years old, and everything since then has been a strange blur. I haven't stopped moving. The world hasn't quit spinning. As I write this, that was 16 years ago. In that time I've lived in nine places, including a stint with my two children in my childhood room with my parents while our stuff moved slowly in a ship container across the Atlantic, closer and closer to Berrien Springs.

Life happens. Is it a cliché? Probably—but it does strike me as a more openhearted cliché than a lot of what Christians tend to spout, and that's why I want to adopt it. It means that nothing is finished or settled, that the mistakes we make don't define us. We move on. We do better. Sometimes we do worse. But life keeps happening, and it offers us these chances.

I STARTED READING Agatha Christie murder mysteries when I was 12, and for a long time my favorite detective was Hercule Poirot. When I got a little older, though, my preference shifted to Miss Marple, an elderly spinster who has lived her entire life in a village and who, in so doing, has developed an uncanny sense of human nature. She is quite unapologetic and even proud of her circumspect life. The lesson seems to be that, if you are paying attention, it doesn't matter *where* you are. You'll notice things, and, little by little, you'll discover glimmers of what really matters. For Miss Marple these cumulate into a broad understanding of what people are capable of, and a clear sense of what drives the human heart. This helps her solve crimes, most often murders, much to the surprise of other people who can't imagine how an old woman who has never been much of anywhere can have any kind of wisdom at all.

I'm a lifelong Adventist and a fourth-generation Adventist. Two of my great-grandmothers were converted in tent "crusades," a fact that stuns me. How could I be linked genetically to not one but two people who would not only attend a tent crusade but actually find it compelling? For a long time I wished that I had been born *anything* but an Adventist. A mosquito, a rhinoceros, an Amway representative—*anything*. I know many people who feel the same way, and even those of us who have long come to terms with the context in which we find ourselves seem to sit with it somewhat uncomfortably. To be an Adventist is to be "less than." People may or may not like what I'm writing, but one thing I know for sure: the very fact that it's been published by a Seventh-day Adventist publishing house will diminish its value, especially among Adventists. All the time, people wonder why anyone would bother to write for Adventists at all. The underlying assumption seems to be that Adventists, as a great singular messy throng, have no taste and that they aren't real people anyway. And of course there's the idea that writing Adventist books is "easier" and doesn't really count.

My response to this is simple: I'm a writer, and being a writer is a lot harder than it looks. First of all, there's the writing. Then there's the chore of trying to get people to *read* what you've written when most of them would rather be Twittering or updating their Facebook status or watching *Celebrity Apprentice*. And if they're going to sit down and bother with a book, they want a *real* book, not rubbish written by some lame Adventist. So my point of view is this: if you want to read what I wrote, I embrace you. I'll take you. You're one of mine. And the thing is, I do occasionally write other kinds of things, but this, this is a book for Adventists because for the most part it deals with things that no other balanced person would care about.

Some people would say that as a group we are insane and that we should talk about some other things once in a while. I couldn't agree more, and at the same time, I find myself somewhat trapped, tied with gossamer strings, to this world—a world in which people will spend two hours debating for the fourteenth time whether wearing a wedding ring means that you consider yourself a harlot or not. I used to hate this and it drove me nuts, but now I find myself strangely charmed by the whole thing. Sure, you could say debating the fine points of caffeine or cinema attendance or brooches versus earrings is a ridiculous waste of energy, and I'm not saying that you're wrong. There is a certain absurdity to all of this. But that's kind of the point. There's a certain absurdity to all of human experience. Isn't there?

The e. e. cummings quote I used to open this book perfectly summarizes my feelings about people, especially the Adventists who are one of the groups of "my" people. I am a member of many groups; many intersecting circles; a virtual walking, whistling, skipping Venn diagram. I am a woman, an American, an honorary Brit, a mom, a sister, a wife, a native of the Pacific Northwest, a slow runner, and a lover of blue glass and of German kitchen knives. I read the *New Yorker* and the *Spectrum* blog and literary fiction and murder mysteries. I am a member of the faculty of the Andrews University School of Education, and I love the people I work with, but a huge number of my friends work across the grass in the College of Arts and Sciences. They give me chocolate and make me laugh. My people are sluggish mountain climbers, those who continually stick their fingers in electrical outlets. Those who call themselves writers but who have to look constantly in reference books to remember how to use the word "whom" and then elect never to use it at all for fear of error. Above all, my people are those who sit uncomfortably prone at times, not completely fitting in anywhere, but humming along all the same. I have the perfect metaphor that describes this state of being: *two chairs*. Allow me to explain.

Before I graduated from college, I told one of my favorite professors of my engagement to a guy I'd met while I was doing a quarter at Newbold College in England. "So I guess I'm moving to the U.K.," I said, happy and nervous and trying to sound braver than I felt.

My professor peered at me over his glasses and said, "For the rest of your life it will be like you're sitting on two chairs—one half of you on one, the other half on the other. It can be done, of course, but it isn't always comfortable." A German national living for decades in the United States, he was, of course, talking about the clash between competing selves and warring cultures. He told me that I would never fully fit into my life in the U.K., but that when I returned home I wouldn't fit in here, either. "I see Germans now," he said, "and I feel critical of them. They look all wrong; their clothes are too tight. But listen to my accent. I'm no American." It didn't take long before I realized exactly what he meant, before I started to cringe at the sound of a loud American voice carrying across the streets of London, calling things quaint, to blanch at the sight of American legs clothed in khaki shorts and super-white socks. And yet I've never stopped being an American. Critical as I can be of Adventists, I've never stopped being one of them, either.

Two chairs. Every time I consider the analogy, I'm always struck with the bold-faced truth of it. My professor wasn't correct merely about the tension of living in and between two cultures. The phrase "two chairs" sums up all manner of tensions in my life, a pervasive feeling of belonging nowhere and of believing competing ideas that cancel each other out. In no part of my life is this more relevant than in the realm people call "spirituality." My main problem, I've concluded, is that I don't use the vocabulary. When talking about whether to take a new job or go on a trip or buy a new sofa, I never make any reference to seeking the Lord's guidance. I don't tell stories about asking God for signs, and when other people do, I never know whether to roll my eyes or seriously admire them for their childlike faith. I live in that flux. All the time. When we do popcorn prayers at work or in other worship services, I never contribute so much as a word. A few months back, I was in a worship in which I was asked to write a haiku about Jesus, and I couldn't think of *anything* I didn't feel silly at the thought of reading aloud to the rest of the group. When I came up blank, my colleagues looked at me in horror— the collective gasp was almost audible. I'm a writer, and I teach writing *for a living.* I'm supposed to be able to write haikus the way some people catch jellybeans in their mouths midair. But if you broke my life down into a pie chart, a decent-sized piece of that pie—enough to make you take your belt out a notch—would be dedicated to staring off into space unable to think of anything.

If there's ever an opportunity for the audience to stand if they love Jesus, I usually sit, although now that I have kids I stand because I don't want them to get the wrong idea. Sometimes I tell people that I will pray for them or for a family member, but when I say the words, they sound horrible and stilted and false. I have no idea why. I'm not *lying.* I do pray for people, but I don't like to *say* that I'm going to. There are a lot of things I don't like to say. For me, most of the time, it's all about the importance of *not* being earnest.

Sometimes I honestly think that the whole schism in society, in church, between "liberals" and "conservatives" is more a matter of vocabulary than anything else. I know a great many people who think that a reluctance to express oneself in typical Christian vernacular is indicative of a deeper problem—and maybe they're right—but in my own life, I'm operating on the following assumptions: (1) I think and speak as I do for a reason; (2) the way I think and speak is an essential part of who I am; (3) my existence as this particular being is of some value; (4) it's important that I utilize my own voice and individuality; and (5) failure to do so would be *really* bad, even tragic. Maybe this sounds bigheaded, as though I think a lot of myself, but it's taken me a long time to be OK with the reality of who I am, so forgive me the trumpeting if you can. I think decades of wallowing in self-loathing are enough to grant a person the right to say, "You know, I'm not really the worst person in the world." Most of the time I feel fortunate that I even have the wherewithal to drag my sorry self around all day every day.

That's why I wrote this book. Sort of. It didn't start out as a book. Each of these essays was an article I wrote mostly during the time I lived in Hemel Hempstead, England, and mostly (with a few exceptions) for a South England Conference youth magazine called *HUB*. During that time I was sitting on two chairs, just as I am now, just as I will likely be for the rest of my life. Forever shifting my weight, trying to get comfortable. Trying not to tip over or embarrass myself. I wish I could say it gets easier, but the truth is that the feeling just gets more familiar. You come to an awkward arrangement with yourself, a truce almost. "OK," you concede, "I'll just sit here then, on these two chairs. I'm fine, really I am."

Another part of you laughs, a low chuckle. "Like you have any choice," it cackles.

"Hey," you say with a shrug. "Life happens."

IN THE REAL WORLD

"YOU SHOULD GET a job at NEXT," someone told me once, referring to a popular British clothing store. "Then you could meet some *real* people."

I didn't immediately know whether I should be a little miffed. For one thing, I don't work primarily to *meet* people, real or otherwise. Insofar as I toil, I do it to save up money to buy my own island and start a utopian dictatorship. Also, on the one hand, I went to college for a really long time. On the other hand, it's not like I majored in particle physics. And actually, NEXT is probably shooting a tad high for me. They wouldn't hire me. No retail experience. No fashion sense.

"I don't mean it in a bad way," she continued. "I just feel sorry for you, having to deal with all these *Adventists* all the time. You need to get out into the real world."

"Sounds ghastly," I said, yawning. "Probably involves taking a 'blue pill,' and discovering that everything I think is real is really just the *Matrix*. I already fell asleep in the movie. Twice. What else do people in the real world do? Get tattoos? If so, I'm actually kind of up for that. Do people in the real world feel pain?"

FUNNY HOW ONCE you tune your antenna the right way, you start picking things up, noticing things more. You get a silver Peugeot, and suddenly everyone else has one too, and now you're always walking toward the wrong car.

The phrase "the real world" has recently begun to bother me. Now that it bugs me—since the universe seems bent on annoying me—everywhere I go, someone's talking about the real world. Or real people. Or reality. Just recently I was watching *Home Alone* with my son, and sure enough, Kevin McAllister's large, piglike, unpleasant brother says—while everyone else is freaking out about poor 8-year-old Kevin being home alone while they're all in Paris—"It'll do the kid some good to get out into the real world."

"What is everyone talking about?" I shouted, throwing a Ping-Pong ball at the TV and missing. *"What* real world?"

For a while, not too many years ago, I was addicted to the British night-time soap *EastEnders.* It has a cast of various colorful characters, and during the time I really liked the show, it was slowly revealing the fact that one young woman's older sister was really her mother. Great stuff. "I love *East-Enders,*" I said to a friend, and she *congratulated* me for this, almost as if I'd announced my short-listing for the Booker Prize.

"That's great!" she squealed. "You have something to talk to *ordinary people* about!"

Christians, and Adventists in particular, stand in thrall of the "real world" and "real people." "Ordinary" people are even better. We actually pride ourselves on our ability to move effortlessly between worlds, to fit in, to be "normal."

"I talked to an ordinary person the other day," you hear people say, "and I told her about how I go to church and everything, and she wasn't even freaked out! It's probably because, unlike most church people, I'm pretty good at fitting into the real world."

In the real world, things are so much more professional.

Real people are nicer.

You'd never survive in the real world.

In the real world the sun always shines. Rainbows burst spontaneously in the sky, like fireworks. Koalas climb right into your lap and let you pet them. The grass is always greener, and your car is always cleaner, in the real world.

Did I mention how professional the real world is? 'Cause as we all know, being "professional" is even more important than being "cute." Sure, it's a totally vague and meaningless term, but so is "the real world." Come on, what twisted dictator would insist that the things we say and think should actually have to mean something?

SPEAKING OF TWISTED dictators, Adolf Hitler apparently said, "If you tell a lie long enough, loud enough, and often enough, the people will believe it."

H'mm. Maybe if Hitler had been smarter, he wouldn't have given away his strategy. He certainly wouldn't have attempted a war on more than one front; we know that. Maybe 60 years ago people believed the things that were said long, loud, and often, but I don't think they do so much now. It's quite the opposite. For me, the longer, louder, and more frequently I hear a statement (whether or not it's an actual "lie"), the more suspect it becomes and the more I begin to take perverse pleasure in poking at it with my number 2 pencil until, if I'm lucky, it explodes.

The things that are really—and undisputedly—true rarely need saying at all. When was the last time you heard anyone argue long, loud, and often that the sky, on a fine day, is as blue as a cornflower?

So what's the deal with "the real world"? What ingenious puppet master is behind the scenes trying to convince us all that (1) there is, in fact, a real world that is somehow distinct from the experiences of certain people (the "clueless") and (2) that anyone who is not judged to be part of this real world is to be mocked and marginalized?

Imagine we have a nice pink balloon. With my semipermanent felt-tip marker I'll carefully write on the fattest part of the balloon, in block capitals, "SOME PEOPLE ARE LESS REAL THAN OTHERS." Sounds sort of stupid when you see it like that. Almost makes the impending pokefest seem redundant and unnecessarily cruel, like flogging a horse that isn't so much dead as unable to lift his head.

As for the puppet master, if not for the part about him being ingenious, I might just suspect former U.S. vice president Dick Cheney. But I tend to suspect him of almost everything. Yeah, including the Lincoln assassination.

THE NEWS a few years back reported on one Judge Seddon Cripps who was so "out of touch" that, during a fraud trial in St. Albans, he asked, "What's a futon?" And he was later baffled by the concept of a "sofa bed," wondering, "How can a bed be turned into a sofa?" The article also cited further evidence that U.K. judges are out of touch with "popular culture" (read here the real world) by pointing out cases of judges who didn't know about Gazza or the Teletubbies or the rock band Oasis.

People like to make each other feel small. As the brilliant Libby Purves pointed out in a column following the report on the hapless Judge Cripps:

"After all, why should a judge, paid to know the law and reflect on public ethics, be expected to riffle through the style supplements and waste good thinking-time on marshmallow media drivel? . . . He's not a contestant in some feeble-minded quiz like *The Weakest Link,* which places cultural dross on the same level as lasting fact."

Who decides what makes a person real or "in touch"? Which committee determines that, to be respected, you must spend hours each week poring over the pages of *People* magazine?

Or better yet: that to be "real" you have to have "issues." You must be "recovering" from something, be it alcoholism or sexual abuse or compulsive gambling. You have to have climbed out of a pit. If you're a Christian, you'll be widely considered clueless and doddering—especially by other Christians who always believe that they, individually, are more "real" than other Christians. You'll never be real unless you loudly proclaim that you used to shoot heroin before you were "born again" and became both a Christian and a "professional."

"That Skippy," people will say, "now he knows a thing or two about the real world."

Nah. What Skippy knows a thing or two about is needles and tourniquets and heating up smack in a spoon. That's not "the" real world. It's "a" real world. It's one of many. As infinite and varied as grains of sand on a long beach—each one worn down from a different kind of shell or rock, each with a slightly different shape and rub, each separate yet touching, clumped together.

Grains of sand come from different shores, washed together by fickle tides. Side by side they sit, each one thinking it's more real than the others. Its journey was longer, harder. Bacteria and viruses and toxic waste from renegade tankers cling to its tiny surfaces.

"I was stuck between a heroin addict's toes for three years," one grain of sand says to another. "Where are you from?"

"I've always lived here," the second grain says wistfully, a little ashamed. It stares out at the vast sea. Every gentle wave is familiar and comforting and hated all at the same time. "Right here on this beach."

"Nice for some!" snorts the first grain. "How can you even relate to the other grains? That grain over there? The one with the blue speck on its side? It lived at the bottom of a saltwater fish tank in a dentist's office! It's had post-traumatic stress therapy. Still wakes up hearing people screaming, the sound of drilling. And you! You don't know a thing about the real world!"

BEING "CLUED IN" or "in touch" or "real" are all variations of the same nonsense. They are meaningless, nonspecific phrases that should drive us all nuts. Yet instead, we buy into them. We repeat them and nod our heads vigorously as if we're quoting Sartre. When people apply these terms to us, we get all giddy with pleasure. We puff our chests out and strut around like Geppetto's Pinocchio! "I'm not a puppet; I'm a real boy!"

Politicians earnestly invoke "the man on the street." What man? I'm always wondering. Which street? What kind of shoes is he wearing? Do they come from NEXT? Because it makes a difference, you know. There are lots of men on lots of streets. Some of them are carrying briefcases. Some are dressed like Native Americans and doing the buffalo dance (yes, even in Hemel Hempstead). Some are vomiting in the gutter. They aren't all the same guy just because they're on the street. They can't be quoted en masse, as if they share a giant ticking brain.

"IF SOMEONE SAID you needed to 'get out into the real world,' what would you take that to mean?" I asked one of my mates the other day. He treats open-ended questions with suspicion.

"Not sure," he answered carefully. "It would depend on who said it."

Well, OK, yeah. Depending on who said it, you could either be a little offended or really upset, but the meaning can't really be doubted, can it? When someone tells you that you need to get out into the real world, they're implying there's something wrong with you. You aren't real enough.

It's a dumb thing to say. How can anyone not be real enough? There are lots of criticisms that can be leveled at people. You can say, "Be punctual." You can say, "Be friendly." You can say, "Beseech." But you can't tell people to be "real." I mean, you can, just like you can run around dressed as a giant chicken, but I'm not going to recommend it or anything.

"Suppose you didn't know the person who said it," I said. "Imagine it was a stranger dressed as a giant chicken. He opens his beak and says in a deep voice, 'You need to get out into the real world.'"

"You've lost me," my friend said.

THE CATCHER IN THE RYE is a book that appeals to many younger people and a few older—mostly crazy—ones, such as Mark Chapman, who shot John Lennon and then immediately sat down and started reading *Catcher*. Holden Caulfield, the book's narrator, is 16 years old and likes the word "phony." To him, almost all other people are phonies. He's the only real one. If you're over the age of 20 and not crazy, he'll irritate you with his tiresome point of view. Part of growing up is recognizing that the only phony you need to worry about is you.

And rarely can you tell what's happening in another person's life. Also, no matter what is happening in their life—even if they have no problems or "issues" at all, even if they sit around reading the Bible in the original Greek all day, they are still real, just as real as anyone else. They've just made different choices. Or had different choices thrust upon them.

"OK," I SAID to my friend who still hates open-ended questions. "What about the whole concept of a real versus an unreal world? What do you think about that? Is there such a thing as a real world, and therefore a corresponding unreal one?"

"Well, sure. There's the world of imaginary numbers, for instance, represented by the lowercase i. In engineering, it's a j. It's the square root of -1. So an imaginary number is a real number times the positive square root of -1."

I stared at him, dismayed. "You're supposed to say 'No.' The answer is no. There's only one world. This is it. Now you've screwed up my thesis. Leave it to an engineer. Useless people."

"Oh," he said. "Sorry."

EVERYONE LIVES AND moves within a context of some kind. Make it work for you. Don't worry about being more "clued in" or "relevant" or "in touch" or "real." Figure out who you are and be the best possible version of that person you can be.

God made each one of us unique and different, and He has a plan for our lives. Quit worrying about what other people consider "real," and let God shape your reality.

WHAT WOULD JESUS
HAVE ME DO?

THE DOORBELL RANG. I answered cautiously, fearfully, as I always do. In my view a ringing doorbell is rarely a positive thing. Occasionally it brings a special delivery, but more often it's a Jehovah's Witness, a telephone company representative, a kid selling shoe polish, or the police asking if I happened to see who broke into the local post office.

This was even worse. A great hulking, stinking, sweaty man with greasy hair and "teeth here and there," as my grandmother would say, stood on my porch. He carried a ladder and a bucket.

"Wash your windows?" he asked.

When startled, I usually agree to whatever is asked of me. (It does depend somewhat on the thing being asked.)

"Um, OK," I hedged. "How much?"

"Fiver," he said.

"Let me see if I have that much."

We struck a deal, the sweaty window-cleaning man and I. He would wash my windows, and I would give him the five one-pound coins I "borrowed" from my son's Peter Rabbit piggy bank. I felt relieved to have gotten rid of him without giving him reason to hold a grudge against me. (He knows where I live!)

Unfortunately, we didn't strike quite the deal I thought we had. I assumed this was a one-time thing. Imagine my surprise when the doorbell rang again about a month later and I opened it to find my unwashed friend and his ladder, again, lounging on my porch.

"Yes?"

"I've washed your windows."

"OK?"

"Just finished."

"You didn't ask me!" is what I wanted to say. Instead, after opening and closing my mouth several times like a gasping guppy, I said, "Right then. So that's five quid?"

"Four's OK."

I fished in my purse and found a pretty cyan-tinged note. "Keep it."

And that's how I got myself a permanent window cleaner, a "domestic," you might say—a member of my household "staff" (making two of us—or three, if you count my husband).

It has been more than a year. The window man appears suddenly, without warning. Sometimes it's the sound of his ladder I hear first: a great crashing, scraping sound as he hoists it up my brick wall. Other times his hulking frame appears in my window, his feet stomping my roses, his zippers scratching the panes. I've almost screamed a few times. Then I pull myself together, collect his payment, and wait for the bell to ring. (I've learned to keep cash on hand.)

He asks me for small things. Can he leave his ladder outside while he goes across to the shops? Can he have a glass of water?

I agree curtly. I'm afraid of being too friendly. When I bring him water, I close the door and tell him to leave the glass on the porch. I don't like my window cleaner. I'm afraid of him. I've thought many times about firing him. It would be so easy. I'd prepare an envelope in advance with five pounds and a polite note. "Thank you very much for the exceptional work you've done, but your services are no longer required." In fact, I'd put 10 pounds in the envelope. Or maybe 20. Enough that I wouldn't feel guilty. Enough that he wouldn't feel the need to slash my tires or wait in the bushes for me as I get out of my car at night.

I can't do it. There's something about him. I can't bear him, right? But at the same time, he looks so dirty and so hungry and so ugly. He reminds me of this awful one-eyed poodle I picked up off the street when I was a kid. The thing was wet and it stank and it had only one eye, for crying out loud, which creeped me out. I didn't want to hold it in my lap, but I held it anyway—all the way to the animal shelter. Someone had to. Even so—I almost worked up the courage to fire the window cleaner when he asked to use my bathroom.

"That's crossing the line," I fumed to anyone who would listen. "What's wrong with him? What kind of lunatic asks to use a total stranger's bathroom? Did he actually expect me to say yes?"

Of course I told him no. I tried to be nice. I looked at him, straight in the eye this time, and I said, "No. I'm very sorry, but I can't let you in the house." I think he understood. I hope so. If not, it doesn't matter. I'm at peace with my decision. I'm a woman alone in a house with two small children. I make no apologies for refusing entry to my home to strangers of any kind, no matter how bedraggled or pathetic. I'm at peace. Sort of.

Whenever he's been around, I feel unsettled for a day or two. I have these odd conversations with myself:

"He's probably a serial killer disguised as a window cleaner."

"You watch too much TV."

"No, I don't."

"Why do you always think everyone is a serial killer?"

"Because I grew up in the Pacific Northwest, that's why. I spent the first 18 years of my life thinking of nothing but Ted Bundy, that's why."

"You're supposed to be a Christian."

"I realize that."

"You're not acting like one. Shouldn't you go the extra mile? Shouldn't you try to help him, more than slipping him a fiver once a month and giving him water? Shouldn't you be transforming his life in some way?"

"How am I supposed to do that?"

"You know, you have to ask yourself that question: 'What would Jesus do?'"

"I don't know what Jesus would do."

Until I moved, I was sure I was going to have this window cleaner for life at a cost of 60 quid a year. Unfortunately, he does a really bad job. He's the worst window cleaner ever. But this isn't about the money. It's not about the windows. This is about me, about what a colossal failure I am. Isn't that what everything is always about?

I KNOW PEOPLE who would probably have given the window cleaner a leaflet—"Why Does God Allow Suffering?" (This would have allowed him to discover why some people have warm homes, clean clothes, wallets stuffed with credit cards and money, and desk jobs—and why he, a window cleaner, is dirty, dentally challenged, hungry, scrounging for coppers, and relying on the fickle kindness of strangers for his supper.)

I'm not a leaflet person. Mind you, I think leaflets can serve a valuable purpose, especially to disseminate medical information and conditions. But can anyone take seriously a leaflet that purports to offer "Quick Answers to

Life's Big Questions" or that claims to tell you "What Happens When You Die" or how to "Find Purpose in Your Life"? A leaflet? Really? Might as well get one of those guys in Piccadilly Circus to write the secret of life on a grain of rice.

I know the people who give out leaflets don't intend to be callous, but a leaflet, to me, is another way of saying, "Sorry about your problem. Here's 20 pence. Call Oprah."

Leaflets. So cold, so clinical. So full of facts and information. Who cares about facts when you're suffering? Who cares about THE TRUTH when what you want is solidarity, the touch of a human hand, a hug, a kind word, a hot cup of tea, or maybe a laugh or two. And some of us need so much more. Who can even begin to know the depths of need in one solitary individual? Sometimes my window cleaner makes me want to cry.

What would Jesus do? I don't know.

I REALLY DON'T. What would Jesus do if He were a woman, if He were a mother, if He were alone in a house, if He'd grown up in a society where rape and murder, while maybe not commonplace, are familiar enough that we rightly fear them?

Maybe Jesus would take His chances.

I've considered that possibility. Maybe these attempts at self-preservation, at the expense of selfless giving, are the essence of what sin is. Maybe I should forget about my safety and that of my children and do good wherever I can. Maybe I should trust God to take care of me.

But surely that's a bit naive. Also, Jesus would know whether someone genuinely needed help or whether they were only pretending in order to gain access to His house. When Jesus died, He did it for a reason. He didn't put Himself in needless danger for nothing. The fact is, I'm not Jesus.

Maybe the real question we should ask ourselves is not so much "What would Jesus do?" but "What would Jesus have *me* do?"

I'm not convinced that Jesus expects me to let a scary stranger use my bathroom. I'm not convinced of that at all. I guess what bothers me more is my own attitude. I don't like this guy. If I don't like him, how can I possibly help him? Aren't my monthly handouts and my glasses of water worthless if I don't have love and concern in my heart? And if I had love and concern, wouldn't I try to get involved in this man's life? Wouldn't I ask him where he lives, ask him if things are OK, try to help him find a better job?

But there's another way to look at it: the window cleaner is a problem for me because his existence in my life makes me uncomfortable with the kind of person I am. I am not able to give what I need in order to feel good about myself. But isn't it possible that I am in fact giving the window cleaner exactly what he needs of me? That is, five pounds a month, drinks of water, and a place to lean his ladder? Not a leaflet or a sermon or a Bible, but a few small, practical things. Things I can do. After all, he's never indicated that he expects me to fix his life. He seems satisfied with the "job," with the water. Maybe it's enough for now, from me.

Or maybe not. Maybe I'm deluding myself. It wouldn't be the first time. While still living in the U.K. and dealing with my window cleaner, I made one decision. The next time my window cleaner came I would give him 10 pounds instead of five. I tried to smile. I tried not to think about Ted Bundy. Or red monkeys. (The truth is that I still thought about Ted Bundy and red monkeys anyway, and I tried to remind myself that it was all in my head.)

SMILING SOCIOPATHS

AFTER SEVERAL YEARS as a teenage monster—during which I cut up my clothes, dyed my hair odd colors, got expelled from outdoor school, almost failed all my subjects, played Lucifer in the church play (a part apparently so tailor-made for me that one member remarked, upon leaving the hall, "That girl will win an Oscar someday!"), got kicked out of the drama club, ran away from home, carried on hunger strikes, tormented my biology teacher with irritating genetic-abnormality-related questions ("If a person were born with only 12 chromosomes, would they be a giant carrot?"), and caused my parents to pack my bags for a detention center—I suddenly, overnight, underwent a transformation. Those of you familiar with Franz Kafka's *Metamorphosis* are no doubt hoping I morphed into a giant insect. Hate to disappoint.

I changed schools when I was 17, moving into a dormitory infested with several hundred extremely perfect girls. They had matching bedspreads. They competed for the best grades. They tripped over each other to be first on the platform at Week of Prayer altar call.

I, on the other hand, decorated my room with a giant pink flamingo poster and an inflatable *T. rex*. I hung out with a few of the weird girls—the ones who choked themselves until they passed out because they were so bored. We would remove the smoke alarms, spray peace symbols on the walls with hair spray, light it, and watch the flames. ("Cool! Do it again! Do a heart this time!") On the first day of school I wore black leather trousers.

My good citizenship grade was a D because I refused to turn my lights off at 10:00 p.m., and I was always missing worship or skipping strict study hall. I didn't care. I spent study hall reading novels with big hulking shirtless men on the covers and raised gold lettering in the titles. The "mean" dean made me scrub mold off the bathroom ceiling with a toothbrush because I missed so many chapels. I'd call my parents and cry and curse them for having sent me to such a Fascist institution, where I felt like a prisoner. "I'm going to eat nothing but lettuce until I die," I'd threaten.

For some reason, halfway through the year this all became a bore. I was tired of fighting and struggling, tired of being a weirdo, tired of my leather trousers sticking to my legs, and tired from staying up all night every night listening to the radiator clang and singing "Hells Bells." I wanted everyone to start liking me.

I started to wear "natural" makeup, long floral dresses, and culottes. I carried a faux crocodile briefcase. I put my hair in a partial ponytail. I wore (fake) wire-rimmed glasses. I studied, made charming conversation with adults, flicked my hair, and smiled.

So I changed my appearance and behavior—this transformation had mostly to do with peer pressure. I became, in short, a smiling teenage sociopath. Bright. Chirpy. Brimming with positive attitude. My final year in school I became a Smart Start counselor—a student with a clipboard and a cheerful Stepford Wives demeanor who lectures the surly new students on the need to clean up their stinky attitudes.

"I hate this school, and I want to kill myself," one girl in my group snarled during a beginning-of-year bonding exercise.

"H'mm," I murmured. "Well, you certainly won't get far with that attitude. Why don't we all join hands and sing 'Kumbaya'?"

Back home—by this time I was living at home again and commuting to school every day and thrilled because this meant I could spend my evenings at the Big Foot Tavern and Pool Hall—I still occasionally showed up late for church to make a grand entrance so everyone could admire me. I believed I could schmooze anyone, anytime. World domination was only a hop, skip, and jump away.

At my church there was a mildly retarded girl named Julie who looked up to me. Julie was a pain. She was always hanging around, calling me on the phone, asking awkward questions—"Becky, how d'ja get a guy?" (A guy? Like, a guy in a "band" who's served 10 to 15 years in San Quentin and sells Amway door to door? No problem. A guy who's polite to your parents, plays the cello, and is going to be a cardiologist when he grows up? No clue.)

But because I was "good," I didn't ever blow Julie off directly, the way I might have back in my bad hombre days. I figured it made me look good, you know, being friends with a retarded person. Being with Julie did, in fact, make me look good by association—smarter, more coordinated, more articulate. It also made me look really kind.

I'd feed Julie all kinds of patronizing advice I gleaned from teen magazines. I'd throw her a few crumbs here and there—thinking I was really doing her a favor by chucking a little of my attention to her.

After I went to college, I didn't see much of Julie. She didn't cross my mind much either, until one day my mom happened to mention that Julie had been picked up in a car by a group of men. They raped her and left her for dead—naked—in a ditch. Traumatized, she spent several months in a mental institution.

It was maybe a year later, a weekend I happened to be home, and I popped into church. I saw Julie at the end of the hall, and I genuinely felt bad about what had happened to her. But being a selfish, empty shell of a person (and also a moron), I thought what would *really cheer her up*—what would *fix everything*—would be a smile and a few kind words from her idol: me. I click, click, clicked my pretty heels across the hall and pasted a devastating smile across my bright-red lips. I called her name in a perky voice. "Julie! Wow, it's so good to—"

I never got a chance to finish that sentence. Julie took one look at me and screamed. She screamed and ran. The heavy glass door crashed behind her as she stumbled in her attempt to get away from me as fast as possible. She ran down a pebbled path strewn with hot-pink rhododendron blossoms—many of them crushed by careless pedestrians. I remember the color because I stood staring at them for quite some time.

"It isn't your fault," my friends immediately assured me. "Who knows what she's thinking? She's psychotic. Probably didn't even know you."

"Hey," someone else no doubt said. "Buck up. It's not like you killed somebody."

I USED TO try to explain Christianity to my former boss. He wasn't impressed by salvation, so I'd tell him about how you need God in order to be a better person.

"I'm already a good person," he'd say. "Aren't you?"

"No," I'd say.

"Come on—you've never done anything *really bad,* have you?"

And if you're talking multiple heads in the freezer—which is on virtually everyone's *really bad* list—no, I've never done anything really bad. My neighbors can sleep easy living next door to me.

If you listen to people talk during the course of, say, a week, you'll be almost certain to hear two phrases at least once: *it's not rocket science* (a phrase that baffles me—what is a "rocket"?), and *it's not like I/he/she killed somebody.*

Nowadays this is the moral yardstick. Give it a few years, and it'll be *It's not like he dismembered anyone* or *It's not like he organized a genocide.* The only people everyone agrees are "bad" are mass murderers and tyrannical dictators. I'm not as bad as Hitler.

This seems to be setting the bar a little low. When you're trying to be good at something—say, tennis—the one thing you don't do is say, "I'm better than Greg Rusedski." If you want to be good, you try to improve. You pay attention to the guy you want to beat—not the guy you could cream on an off day. You can't afford to forget your weak serve.

So why, when it comes to character—perhaps the most important thing we have—are we so complacent, so certain that we're "pretty good"?

It's all about liking yourself. I, however, think life gets interesting in the moments you hate yourself. These are the times God taps you on the shoulder and says, "Sunshine, you know I love you, but what were you thinking?"

THE EXPERIENCE WITH Julie taught me a valuable lesson—though I struggle to explain exactly what that lesson was. That you shouldn't be phony? That's not quite it. Maybe this is why I like stories more than sound bites. There are things in that story—no, in that scene, the way it plays in my head—that can't be expressed any other way. Calling it a lesson doesn't do it justice.

Anyway, learning lessons isn't the same thing as changing. It wasn't like I woke up the next day a new person—sincere and caring. It isn't as though I've ever awakened as the person I'd like to be—though at least I've (so far) never wakened as a giant insect.

THE FIRST STEP is admitting you have a problem. Then what's the next step? 'Cause the real problem most of us have is that we *like* the things that are wrong with us. We think they're what make us special. We gleefully point out our shortcomings—because we don't think they're actually bad, the way everyone at a job interview, when asked, "What is your greatest flaw?" says, "I'm a workaholic." It's the flaw that's not a flaw. And you look so honest admitting it!

Sometimes I feel guilty for being such a rotten, psychopathic teenager and putting my parents through agony, and other times I am inordinately pleased with myself, with my individuality, my creativity, my sheer brilliance, the fact that I alone had an inflatable *T. rex* in my room.

Many people pride themselves on their cynicism. This is seen, somehow, as a synonym for intelligence. Jesus, however, told us to be like little children. Not cynical. Not phony. Open. Honest. Loving. Pure.

These qualities sound so boring. Who wants to be open and honest when you can be clever and conniving instead? When you can be smarter than other people or ask hard-hitting questions? Good people are simpletons. How often do we roll our eyes when we hear a potential date described as "nice"? We prefer San Quentin Sam and his base guitar. We want to be smart, hip, edgy, sexy—anything but nice. *I'm not a nice person, but I'm OK. It's not like I killed somebody.*

God expects more of us. We should expect more of ourselves. We should demand more—the way we demand more fries in our cardboard containers.

One way is this: don't ever say you're good enough (in a moral sense) as you are. Don't allow yourself to think it. Don't be smug or complacent. This isn't about perfectionism. I'm not talking about salvation—I know God is more than capable of making up for my flaws. This is about me trying to see if I can cultivate the better parts of my nature rather than watering and obsessively fertilizing my nasty bits.

Allow yourself, once in a while, to really feel some shame. Remind yourself, every so often (not so much that you fall into a crippling depression), of one of those occasions you've seen yourself (if only for an instant) for who you really are. One of those memories that makes your cheeks burn. One of those moments that make you realize a Savior might be something you need after all.

BIG BOXES

FOR MANY YEARS, until I grew bored of it, my favorite thing on TV was *America's Next Top Model*. I suppose I should feel ashamed to admit this, but I have no shame. The show fascinated me, and I guess as long as I'm being honest I should admit that I still watch reruns of the series occasionally when they run back-to-back on Sundays. *Shh.*

My enjoyment of the show could be in part because, when I was a teen, I wanted to be a model. I wanted to be a model so badly that I worked for three months at a place called the German Retirement Home—serving cabbage rolls and tolerating old men who were always asking me to button their trousers—to pay for modeling school.

Yep. You wouldn't know it to look at me, but I'm a genuine graduate of the Vincenzo Morini School of Modeling, which is obviously a name I made up—not to protect the real modeling school so much as because I can't remember the real name. But it was something cheesy. I learned how to walk and how to apply makeup. I also learned all the things that are (physically) wrong with me. Just a brief sampling: My knees are "a problem." I have a jutting chin. I have a long face. My nose is too big. I have freckles. I have "avant-garde" dress sense (fashion-speak for no dress sense whatsoever). And if you look closely at my eyes (and please don't—it freaks me out), you'll see that one of my irises is higher than the other.

My graduation from modeling school involved a truly appalling catwalk show in which I wore, among other things, a matching yellow leather skirt and jacket with a chain belt (this was 1987). My parents had to witness this, poor things. I can only imagine the pain it must have caused them: the horror at the realization that their only daughter was a shameless—and tacky—twit. We never speak of this catwalk show. Ever.

Of course, modeling school was worth every penny. As a good friend recently pointed out: "Look how well you walk." Indeed. I hardly ever fall down.

I quickly got over wanting to be a model. I'm much too pragmatic to cling for long to vain hopes. Like Aesop's fox and his "sour grapes," I can sneer at something forever out of my grasp.

And sneer I often do as again and again the contestants on *America's Next Top Model* say such things as "I want to make something of myself." They put medical careers and other sorts of jobs on hold to pursue this dream. Clearly they aren't interested in making just "something" of themselves. It has to be something very specific. It has to be fame and validation on a Tyra Banks–type scale. Most of them will never come close to achieving this.

Sometimes I stop sneering long enough to feel sorry for the girls. For all of us, really. For everything we could be and don't choose to be because we're too busy pursuing something else.

I HAVE A Big Box of Grievances. It's a virtual box. One I store in a dusty corner of my mind right next to my Pile of Good Intentions and across the corridor from my Bag of Major Regrets.

My favorite grievance is how the dean of women at my college refused to give me a reference to attend Newbold College for one quarter because I was, as she put it, "Very, *very,* unattractive."

Perhaps this requires some context, so let me explain. I was 21. I'd given up on being a model, but I remained a devoted reader of *Vogue.* I followed all the fashions. It was 1993. Miniskirts were big—or shall I say small. Short hair was in: think Linda Evangelista. This might be a good time to mention that when I was a child—in the seventies—my mom cut my hair short like the ice-skater Dorothy Hamill. People thought I was a boy. At 21 I felt I needed to compensate for the lack of hair. Translation: I wore a lot of makeup.

"We tolerate you here," she continued. "But I don't know how they feel about this kind of thing over there."

"What kind of thing?" I asked, near tears.

She sighed. "Like I said, you often go around looking *very* unattractive. Very unattractive indeed."

I returned to my room, flung myself on my bed, and wailed for hours. My roommate was so angry and so loyal that she dressed up like the dean— boxy business suit, scarf, four brooches, stiff middle-age-woman hair, and streaks of war-paint rouge on her cheeks. She stomped to the dean's office and demanded to know whether she looked "attractive." I will always love her for that.

Everything turned out fine. I got one of my history professors to give me a reference instead. I left for Newbold College one month later. My roommate and I backpacked all over Europe that summer and schemed about all the different insulting postcards we might send to our dean.

In the end I was too chicken to confront her—either in insulting postcard fashion or in a reasonable adult conversation. I've been left, as a counseling professional might put it, without "closure." And here I am, 12 years later, still upset. Still clenching my fists and having imaginary conversations with the dean in my head: "I'll have you know, I went to modeling school."

How dare she call me unattractive? It's the worst thing the woman could possibly have said. I've wondered about this over the years. Why does it bother me so much? Why do I feel like I've been kicked in the stomach every time I recall that awful scene?

Here's a hypothesis: Anything else she might have leveled at me, I could have denied. I could have proven her wrong. If she'd said I was stupid, I would have showed her my grades. If she'd said I was selfish, I would have run down and volunteered at the nearest homeless shelter just to show her. But how can you prove that you aren't unattractive? Especially if you're kind of afraid you are?

Let's face it, it's not enough for your mom to think you're cute. Your friends won't tell you the truth—they like you for your sense of humor. And you can't believe men—they'll say anything.

That brings us back to the question Why do all these goofy girls want to be models? As a former and, some might argue, continuing goofy girl, I'll take a shot at an answer. I wanted to be a model, because if I were a model, I would have—ladies and gentlemen of the jury—irrefutable, in-your-face proof that I was beautiful and that I was worth something. If no one can question your value, if no one dares call you "unattractive" (read "worthless"), you are so safe.

Or so a lot of us think. But consider this: a well-known fashion designer once said of Cindy Crawford, "The most famous woman in the world, and she's just a clothes hanger."

Ouch. If I were Cindy, that would be right at the top of my Big Box. Maybe being Cindy wouldn't be as easy or as safe as it looks.

MY BROTHER IS six feet eight inches tall. He can slam-dunk a basketball. I'm five seven. I cannot. But I used to think I could. I'd argue with my brother for hours on the basketball court, in between huffing and puffing and hurling myself toward the basket, only to fall about three feet short of the rim.

"I just need more practice," I'd say.

He'd laugh. "You'll never dunk that ball. You're too short. Also, you're a girl."

"How can you say I'm too short?" I'd shout. "I can do anything I set my mind to, right? I'll go to the gym and do 500 leg presses every day. Or 1,000. I'll do a lot. My legs will be like human springs. You just watch. I'll do it. What about that short guy in the NBA? Whassis name? And don't get me started on the girl thing."

"You're no Spud Webb," my brother said. "Why not do something you're good at?"

The kid used to be so dumb I could steal M&Ms from right under his nose. "One for you, one for me . . ." I'd chant, while slipping two or three under my finger toward my own pile. If he asked why my pile looked bigger, I'd say, "It's not bigger—it's just more spread out." The kid turned out to be a genius: Why not do something you're good at? Good question. And here's another one: Why not *value* the things you're good at?

THERE IS NO point in berating people for being looks-conscious. This seems to be part of the way we're made. We respond to beauty. We value it. We reward it. It is no less shallow to value someone for their intelligence or their personality or their sense of humor than it is for their looks. These attributes are just as arbitrary and just as outside our control as the features on our faces. Why is it acceptable to say you love someone for their sense of humor, but not for their looks? It's not like there's some virtue in being funny—something the person has cultivated through merit. We're not all Rowan Atkinson any more than we're all Naomi Campbell—no matter how hard we try. And we can't all be everything. So why do pretty people want to be smart and smart people want to be funny and funny people want to be pretty? And why aren't the small validations, the little things, enough to make our lives feel worthwhile?

I remember thinking that once I got my degree I'd have things figured out. I'd be, you know, a historian. Big deal, right? Not really. The euphoria lasted about two days. It's been like that with everything I thought would make my life complete. I get it, I get used to it, and it loses its luster. I thought

I'd be so cool if I could design magazines and posters and adverts and logos. Now that I can, I reckon a well-trained gorilla could do the same.

I read somewhere that one of the early and more successful of the *America's Next Top Model* winners, Yoanna House, is mocked by other "authentic" models for being from a reality TV show. Winning isn't all it's cracked up to be. In my experience there are only one or two things that are. Having someone love you is so all cracked up that if you filled it with water it would leak all over the floor.

I WAS SASHAYING down the corridor in Newbold's Murdoch Hall one morning in a pair of clunky platform shoes, wearing a floral granny dress and an artistically tattered cardigan. I met a guy near the water fountain. "Those are the dumbest looking shoes I've ever seen," he said.

Reader, I married him.

Someone asked him just the other week what it was that first attracted him to me, and he didn't say it was my spirituality or my stunning wit or my gentle nature.

"Dude," he said. "I thought she was hot."

"Shallow!" I hear someone screaming. No, it ain't. At any rate, I'll take it. I'll add it to my Big Box of Miracles. I keep it stacked right at the top of my teetering pile of grievances, disappointments, and insecurities. I figure if it gets heavy enough it will flatten everything underneath.

CHAV SCUM

DURING THE TIME I lived in the U.K., I learned a whole new vocabulary. Just to give you a sampling of the kinds of words I learned, I'll offer two examples: *inveigle,* for which I scoured the I section of the dictionary so I wouldn't have to admit having acquired only the slightly less intellectual *chav.*

Inveigle hasn't traveled far out of page 960 in the *New Oxford Dictionary*, but chav has certainly been to town and back a few times, at least in the U.K. Newspaper headlines. Book covers. TV specials. Web sites. *Chavscum.co.uk* is the one that I—unable to resist anything containing the word *scum*—was instantly drawn to.

A chav, for those of you even more out of touch than I, is a person—usually young—who wears athletic gear, cheap gold jewelry, and white trainers. Chavs hang out in malls. They are materialistic and have no values. They're either on the dole or they work in factories or at McDonald's. Chavs Are Ruining Britain! the headlines used to scream, and probably still do. Here in the U.S., a comparable term is probably "trailer trash."

At first this media hysteria made me yawn. Am I really supposed to be alarmed that people are allowed to wander the suburban landscape wearing "prison" white shoes or too much gel in their hair?

My brain is mostly an alarm-free zone. I'm not bothered about fat people or gamblers or Jerry Springer. I believe the fewer things that "offend" you, the happier you'll be. It's nearly impossible to offend me. I'm like one of those palace guards who won't laugh. Go ahead, try to make me.

But while I rarely succumb to alarm, I often indulge in a bit of smugness. *There are too many tacky scumbags around*, I've thought. I noticed this when I first arrived in Britain expecting a charming cast of doddering, tweed-clad, marrow-growing villagers from an Agatha Christie book. Instead I got guys in boots and orange-lined bomber jackets shouting and pee-ing in public places. "The English," I'm always telling people, "are not as classy as you might think."

And now I had a name for it! I started taking note of all the "inferior" people in my neighborhood while walking down the street. Chav. Chav. Chavette. Big fat chav. Little kid chav. Dear Lord, thank You that I am not like that girl with the thigh-high vinyl boots.

As I see a 15-year-old "loser" sitting at the bus stop blowing smoke in her baby's face, I think to myself, *I would never be like that.* Of course, at that point and time a voice (maybe my conscience?) kicks into gear and answers with a sly giggle, "Wanna take a gander at some video footage, darling? And doncha worry now—I got plenty more where this came from."

"Fast-forward. No, nope, gone too far. Rewind. Right there. Freeze-frame. Wanna ID the person stepping outta that car?"

Stubborn silence.

"Alrighty then. The person stepping out of the car is you, Becky Sue. Wanna describe what you got on?"

More stubborn silence.

"You're wearing a purple track suit and big fake gold earrings. Zoom in to the hand. You got tacky gold rings on each finger. One of them is shaped like the great state of Texas. Remember how you wanted a leather jacket that looked like an American flag?"

"I didn't buy it, did I?"

Snorting, derisive laughter. "You didn't buy the jacket 'cause you couldn't afford the cursed thing."

This voice in my head doesn't like me to lie. It is always demanding this complete, exhausting, demoralizing honesty. It wears me down until I con-fess, wasted and screaming, to anything it demands. So stuff it—yes—I've worn some very ill-advised clothes and jewelry in my life. For a full five years I spelled my name Bekii. I had a job that required me to ask, "Would you like fries with that?" I owned a Gucci bag. I named my cat Alexis. Need I continue, or is the above enough to convict me of being no better than the next person?

"Well?" the voice (maybe it's God?) demands. "Whatcha gotta say for yourself? What's the air like up there on that high horse? Little thin, huh? Not enough oxygen gettin' to your brain? Just who do you think you *are,* anyway?"

OK, SO CHAVS are too materialistic and have bad taste. They use their brains somewhat less than they should. They have far too high an estimation of David and Victoria Beckham. These are not admirable traits, but chavs are hardly Papa Doc Duvalier of Haiti. They aren't especially hurting anyone. And what do middle-class people care about? Home ownership. Home renovations. House prices. Private school for their kids (presumably to shield them from chavs). As values go, are these actually better? Or even different? Why? How? Aren't they all about appearances—more or less?

Watching the English, by Kate Fox, points out that class has nothing to do with your occupation or with how much money you have. It has everything to do with (1) how you speak and (2) what your tastes are. Read it. If you're English, you may laugh with recognition at yourself and others. If you're not, you'll probably just laugh.

As entertaining as class differences are, does it really matter whether you match your curtains to your sofa? Whether you prefer a living room "suite" or a hodgepodge of ill-matching random items? Whether you call it a settee or a sofa?

Nobody much likes to admit this, but our "tastes" and "preferences" and "interests" are just things to keep us occupied until we die. Nothing more.

I OCCASIONALLY HEAR church people talk about how they hope to attract and convert professionals. This term, like many terms, confuses me senseless. I don't understand what it means. A professional what? Prostitutes are referred to as "professionals." There are professional athletes. In this context, a professional is simply someone paid to do something—as opposed to the amateur athlete, perhaps equally skilled but forced to work the off-season in a stifling accounts office. Technically, then, anyone who is paid to work is a professional something. Except that's not strictly what people mean when they use this term, is it? I've heard it put more bluntly from people hoping to attract "those earning in excess of $100,000 per year."

Is a professional someone who wears a tie or heels to work? Someone who uses a computer? Is it a member of one of the "professions"—a doctor, lawyer, chartered accountant? Or is it just someone we deem "respectable"? (I use a computer when I "work," but I tend to wear mostly pajamas. What does that make me? Maybe I'd just as soon not know.)

Perhaps non-Christian journalists can be forgiven for their rampant and hostile labeling of an entire class of people, but what's our excuse? Have we forgotten that Jesus didn't exactly favor the company of "respectable" people?

YESTERDAY I READ *The Velveteen Rabbit* to my 5-year-old son. "This is the greatest children's book ever written," I sobbed as I choked through the book's explanation of what it means to be "real." "By the time you are Real, most of your hair has been loved off, and your eyes drop out and you get loose in the joints and very shabby. But these things don't matter at all, because once you are Real you can't be ugly, except to people who don't understand."

"That *is* the greatest children's book ever," my son said nervously.

"Wanna hear it again?"

"No thanks."

The purpose of life is to become real. When you're real, you never look stupid, except to people who don't understand. OK, that's a lie (inveiglement?)—you will often look stupid, but it doesn't matter. You can wear white trainers. You can wear Birkenstocks. You can wear three-inch red heels. Go barefoot. Whatever. When you're real, you aren't defined by your shoes, nor is anyone else defined by theirs. They're only shoes.

I'm not a psychologist (I don't even play one on TV), but I still have a little exercise to help you become your authentic self. Go buy your own idea of the ugliest and most humiliating outfit there is, and wear it in public. Don't wash or comb your hair. Go without makeup. If you're a man, go without whatever men use to make themselves attractive (deodorant?). Wear the ugly outfit until you forget you're wearing it. When you know who you are, even when you don't look cool, that's when you become real.

The worst thing that can possibly happen is that someone snaps your picture and posts it in the gallery at chavscum.co.uk. If they do, shrug. Someone has to make the people laugh.

WHATEVER SHOES YOU wear, if you're going to aim for something (and we all do), this is what it should be: You want to see the best in people and in situations. You want to remain open to new experiences and to treat life as an endlessly interesting experiment. You want to be honest about who you are and willing to see the humanity in others—even if they're shouting and wearing polyester.

You'll be a boring person if you box and label people because then you'll be forced to box and label yourself. You'll become stiff and judgmental. You'll start referring to other people as "common" in a high, whiny voice. You'll try to be respectable or cool (or whatever you call that thing everyone wants to be) rather than trying to be who God calls you to be—His disciple. When you're old, you'll knock your head against the wall, wondering why you always worried about the wrong things. Don't analyze your shoes to see whether they're cool: put them on and go somewhere. Do something.

"THE MOST DANGEROUS enemy of truth and freedom [is] the solid, unmoving cattle of the majority," wrote Ray Bradbury in *Fahrenheit 451*. Ain't that the truth? Everybody screaming at you, telling you what to think, who to be, what to respect, what not to wear. If you do nothing else in your life, *resist*. And be honest. And don't be afraid. This is so much harder than it sounds, not because by resisting you risk being singled out, but because as God's followers we are called to be who God made us to be, regardless of what other people think about us.

Feel free to resist me too, if you can, but there's little point, because my arguments are, as usual, airtight. Anyway, when the revolution comes, I think you'll find it advantageous to be on my side. OK, that's the voice in my head—or maybe it's the radio operator from my spacecraft telling me it's time for my medication.

PEACE, CHILD

"I do not want my house to be walled in on all sides and my windows to be stuffed. I want the cultures of all the lands to be blown about my house as freely as possible. But I refuse to be blown off my feet by any."—Mahatma Gandhi.

THE MAN WAS asleep on a soft mat on the floor of a crude hut. Curled on his side like a baby, he'd fallen asleep in the house of a cherished friend after a sumptuous meal and an evening spent telling stories around a warm fire. So comfortable and at peace was this man that he didn't even stir as a dozen or so men crept single-file into the hut, quietly surrounding the man as if preparing for a friendly game of farmer in the dell. Each man carried a spear and wore a fierce expression. One or two of them carried pitch-burning torches. When they were all assembled in their rightful places, someone cleared his throat or made some other small sound. The sleeping man stirred. Someone shuffled his feet. All eyes watched the man, waiting for the moment he opened his eyes. The man licked his lips, sleepily opened his eyes, rolled onto his back . . . and then sat bolt upright, eyes suddenly wide with fright as he took in the sight of the circle of men, immediately understanding what it meant. The circle of men erupted into laughter. Gotcha! Fade to black. Cut to strips of human flesh barbecuing on a large outdoor grill, the entire village lined up, laughing maniacally, bottles of A1 sauce in hand.

"I don't get it," I whispered to the girl sitting next to me in the youth hall. "They ate him?"

BACK SOME 20-ODD years ago, watching a film at home or anywhere outside a cinema was a big deal and required advanced planning, rental equipment, and perhaps a degree in engineering—or at the very least the ability to sort and plug wires without throwing your bowl of popcorn through the window in a fit of rage. Because of the logistical challenges, you knew with certainty that any teacher or youth leader who came bursting through the doors with a reel-to-reel projector or TV/VCR on a wheeled cart was about to change your life. Anything they showed us was burned forever into our minds.

The film *The Peace Child,* based on a book of the same title by Don Richardson, is about the Sawi people of New Guinea. As of 1962, when Richardson and his wife, Carol, went to live among them, the Sawi were cannibal/headhunters who fought among themselves. In this twisted culture where values seemed turned back-to-front, murder was considered a good thing. But not just ordinary murder. In order to be "a legend maker," a Sawi would first pretend to make friends with someone, luring him into complacency, and then he would kill him once he was fully convinced of the authenticity of the friendship.

These same people, prizing treachery as the greatest good, laughed themselves into fits when the missionaries relayed the story of Judas' betrayal of Jesus with a kiss. The way they saw it, Judas was the hero of the story, "a legend maker." If the story of Judas and Jesus and the kiss were made into a cowboy movie, Judas would wear the white hat and ride off into the sunset with the pretty woman.

I was 13 years old, and it had never before occurred to me that there might be more than one way to see the story of Judas. *Never.* It seemed to me, at that still-innocent time of life, that there were such things as good and bad and that everyone—all humans everywhere, even the ones who stuck bones through their noses—understood these concepts in the same way I did.

Even if a person did bad things—such as sauté other people's organs— he would be nothing more than an anomaly, someone the rest of his village tries helplessly to explain. "I raised him with values," his mother would sob on an evening news program, wiping her nose with a wadded handkerchief. "Napkin on his lap at mealtimes, no more than a half hour of television a day—and never anything violent. He called his elders 'sir' and 'ma'am.' Did his homework on time. Never gave me or his father a minute of trouble."

People could be bad, sure. But societally sanctioned badness? Bad as good? Hate as love? The big chief handing out medals to those who tricked and ate their friends? Was it possible that words were nothing more than jig-saw pieces—part of a giant puzzle in which any two pieces fit together and nothing has to be any particular way and no matter what you do, you create a picture?

But the more I considered the idea, the more it started—strangely—to please me. I've always liked surprises—the little shock you feel when you discover a truth wholly unexpected. *Eureka!* Life is not what you thought. *Eureka!* The impossible was possible after all. There were people in the world who were *nothing like me*. They didn't care about the same things, weren't frightened or repelled by the same things. They were something else entirely. What? Is a person who prizes treachery, death, and cannibalism even a person? Like I am a person? Human? What makes you human?

"Don't be a fool," a friend answered when I asked the same question. "Your DNA makes you human."

"What makes you a Christian?"

"Giving up your sins and following Jesus."

"But what if, to you, your sins are good? What if you're taught that wrong is right? What about people who bury suspected adulterers to the neck and stone them, fathers who murder their own daughters in 'honor' killings, tribes who perform ritual sacrifices? They do these things because they believe they are good—even required. How are people supposed to become Christians if even their thoughts are so corrupt that they don't know the difference between right and wrong?"

"I don't know. What happened with the Sawi people?"

"Are you kidding? It's been more than 20 years. Anyway, after they ate the first guy, I think I went to the bathroom and locked myself in one of the stalls. I was too scared."

CHRISTIANS, WE ARE told, are supposed to transcend the cultures we are born into. We are not merely to reflect the values of our parents and societies, but to embody the character of Christ. In the old days, whenever Western Christians converted "natives," those natives would begin to wear white shirts with collars and ties. They'd sing hymns. In the books I read as a child growing up, the people of Burma would stop chewing betel nut, and they'd get rid of the pigs that lived under their raised huts. That was how you became a Christian, and that was why it was always easier to convert people who already wore white shirts and lived without pigs or dark-red juice dripping from their teeth onto their chins. You don't notice the extent to which the person you are is informed by your culture until you leave it and enter foreign territory where the behavior of others jars you.

As a kid I was fascinated with other cultures, with the clothes and cus-

toms and languages of other people. On trips with my family I'd busy myself in the corner of the hotel room with the Gideon Bible, copying John
3:16 in the curly script of Sinhalese or Tamil, the elegant scrawl of Arabic,
or the boxy simplicity of Hebrew or Korean. I spent hours pouring over
the section of the encyclopedia that dealt with native costumes, admiring
the bright silks of Asia, the lace of Spain, the palm fronds of the South Pacific. One of my greatest disappointments was finding a girl from Zambia
who joined my third-grade class dressing in blue jeans and a T-shirt. Still,
I wanted particularly to be her friend—to be the friend of anyone who
came from anywhere else. The endless variation among people seemed
wonderful to me.

The difference between being a child and being an adult is that when
you're a child you never have to think about anything horrible for very long.
Horrors, injustices, these roll off you like water off an otter's fur. Things can
appear to you as nothing more than curiosities—you don't have to deal with
them. They don't confront you, forcing you to make choices, to take uncomfortable stands.

*"What sets worlds in motion is the interplay of differences, their attractions
and repulsions. Life is plurality, death is uniformity. By suppressing differences and
peculiarities, by eliminating different civilizations and cultures, progress weakens life
and favors death. The ideal of a single civilization for everyone, implicit in the cult
of progress and technique, impoverishes and mutilates us. Every view of the world
that becomes extinct, every culture that disappears, diminishes a possibility of
life."—Octavio Paz.*

NOT TOO LONG ago I came upon an article in a newspaper about a
young woman of a lower-caste family somewhere in the Indian subconti-
nent. She was the first in her family to receive an education and, as such,
was the pride of her parents. The men of another family in the same village, unhappy that one of the young woman's brothers was interested in
their sister, decided to bring "shame" upon the entire family by kidnap-
ping the educated young woman and raping her. After this news came to
light, the school, which had recently offered the woman employment as a
teacher, revoked their offer. They did not want to be "tainted" by association with this "scandal."

I read the article several times over, just to make sure I understood, because I couldn't understand. How is it possible that people can think that by acting in a dishonorable, criminal way they are bringing "shame" on another person? Weren't they, in fact, bringing shame only upon themselves? Although I am familiar with this idea and have heard many, many stories of this kind, they never fail to shock me a little. How is it possible for people—human, in their DNA, just like me—to look at the same set of facts and reach such different conclusions?

My 13-year-old self thrilled a little at the possibility of pluralism, the way there could be so many answers to the same question, endless facets to the same bit of cut crystal. But my 35-year-old self feels tired and a little sick at how people are. At how wrong the world is. Let me put it this way: maybe sometimes there are some possibilities of life that should disappear, and quickly (don't spare the horses)—without weeping or violins playing. Not everything is valuable or worth preserving just because it happens to be a part of someone's culture. A difference that includes violence or cannibalism is not wonderful or interesting. It is *pain*. It is a prison. It isn't what we were created for.

I WAS CURIOUS about how *The Peace Child* ended, so I googled it on the Internet. Turns out the Richardsons finally found a way to get through to the Sawi—a concept within their culture that gelled with the reality of Jesus. This was the idea of the peace child—the only guarantee that all Sawi would honor. It was the exchange of infants between villages. While any other form of murder was sanctioned, the killing of a peace child was not. Peace reigned as long as the peace child lived. Richardson used this idea—that Jesus is the peace child who will live forever, establishing eternal harmony among people—to get through to this tribe of people. Many of them became Christians as a result. Probably they started wearing ties and singing "Amazing Grace," but none of that matters. What matters is that even in this depraved, upside-down culture there remains the essence of an idea that leads to Jesus. And that, along with DNA, is what makes us human—this tangible link we all have with God.

It is OK for us to be different. In fact, it's more than OK—it's the way it is. The reality is that the world is full of varying cultures. We all come from different backgrounds, and what is acceptable to me would seem strange to those in India, and vice versa. We are different, whether we like it or not—but we are not called to complacency. Jesus offers us true freedom from everything that might keep us from being the people we were created to be. This includes aspects of our various cultures that are not right. Socrates famously remarked that the "unexamined life is not worth living." We all come to Christianity with our own cultures and viewpoints, our own way of seeing the world, but none of that excuses us from the task of trying to see the world as Jesus does. The mixture of beauty and ugliness that the world offers swirls around us like a colorful tornado, and we stand still in the midst of it all. *I will not be blown off my feet,* we say, and close our eyes.

ARCTIC SWAMP MONSTER

A LONG TIME ago a friend and I were skiing fast through the trees on a crude trail. Screaming. Whooping. Having fun. It was nearing dark. At some point I lost my balance and fell on my face. I slid several meters before I clawed myself to a standstill. One of my skis had come off, so I trudged up the hill to retrieve it. As I popped my heel into the grip, I noticed, out of the corner of my eye, something moving.

It's too bad no one timed me, because I'm pretty sure I'm the legitimate 1988 downhill champion of the world. There's nothing to make you move like cold fear. Even after I was in the lodge with a hot cup of chocolate and a big plate of fries, I didn't stop shaking—not for a long time. I couldn't believe what I saw.

As it turns out, not many people believed me.

In fact, just a few weeks ago I was telling my friend the story. We've known each other for a little more than five years. I felt it was time to take our relationship to the next level, so I dropped this bomb out of the blue. Of course, it bore no relationship to anything we'd been discussing, but nothing fazes this girl, so I thought I would see if she believed my story.

"This one time I was skiing in the woods, and I saw a pale white hand reaching out of a frozen pond," I told her.

"Yeah, right," she smirked. "And just what exactly were you smoking in those woods?"

For the record, I wasn't smoking anything. But this is the kind of reaction I get anytime I share what I saw. Ridicule. Derision. Offers of professional counseling. Urine tests. My father is the only one who took me seriously enough to insist that I take him back to the place where I saw the hand, only by then it was summer; and everything was different. There were no frozen pools. I couldn't find the right spot. I can offer no proof that the hand ever existed. I can't prove that I'm not crazy.

Other people suggest alternate explanations. They tell me that what I saw was not what I saw. Probably a floating mitten or someone playing a practical joke.

"Maybe you were on *Candid Camera*," one person offered.

"Why didn't you help?" other people ask. "Someone probably fell in and was trying to get out."

Clearly, these people have never seen a single episode of *Scooby-Doo*. There's no way I'm pulling an Arctic swamp monster from his murky home. Anyway, I'd been skiing that trail all afternoon. There had been no one else in sight. And any good outdoorswoman knows hypothermia will kill you in 20 minutes—the hand was not a living person. At least this is what I tell myself . . .

Maybe it was a dead body or a mannequin. Except I swear it was reaching. Fingers grasping. Also, there were no missing person reports. I've spent years trying to make sense of what I saw, and I simply can't. I cannot make it rational.

Sometimes, whether you like it or not, you just see things.

EVEN MY BEST friends, people who I'm pretty sure would describe me as trustworthy, don't believe my story. It's not that they think I'm lying. They think I'm mistaken. They're willing to concede that I think I saw a hand reaching from a pond, but they don't accept the objective reality of that hand. They don't live in the kind of world where hands reach out of ponds. I understand that entirely. I don't live in that kind of world either—it's just unfortunate for me that I saw it. Once you've seen something, you have three choices: you can lie, you can tell the truth, or you can shut up and never mention it.

We, who have "seen" God, have the same three choices. We often get the same reactions from our friends when we mention our faith in God. They may not laugh at us. They may, in fact, respect our beliefs as our beliefs—but they don't accept the objective reality of God. They're willing to concede that we think we saw God, but that's it. Or maybe they'll agree that they too believe in God, but they won't join our church. It seems to be pretty well accepted by now that this is our fault. We Christians are jerks. We're too judgmental. We're irrelevant. We're unprofessional.

Let's suppose I decide to start a religion, and this religion is contingent upon my getting people to believe that white hands really do reach out of ponds. What would I have to do to make them "believe"?

Would it help if I were cooler? What if I were more professional, had a better job, a business suit instead of flannel pajamas? What if I drove a Range Rover? What if I hired a slick venue from which to broadcast my beliefs? if I picked my nose less? What if I were really nice? Would any of this make a difference? I'll go ahead and break the tension: I say that it would not. I might get people to come along for the party or the free food. My friends might pitch in to support me, but they probably wouldn't "believe" in the white hand.

If you want someone to believe in icy hands reaching out of snowy ponds, maybe you have to show them. Maybe they have to see for themselves. Of course, as we've already observed, this can get dicey. Snow thaws. Landscapes change. And, not to be too confusing, but even seeing isn't always believing. I, for instance, don't actually believe in any kind of monster. Then again, I don't disbelieve in monsters either.

I'm 33, and I've lived the majority of my life in two small geographical areas. What do I know about the world, really? Not much. And I change my mind a lot, too. And I believe things that are mutually exclusive. This is called cognitive dissonance. It's very common and doesn't infringe much on your life, unless, for some reason, you're called upon to explain what you believe. This, I'll bet, is why most of us don't care too much for witnessing. It's embarrassing to realize how incoherent we truly are.

THERE ARE MANY reasons to believe in God. There are also many reasons not to believe in God. Each one of us is born knowing nothing. Through our lives we are told stories by other people. We are told how the world works, what the world is, what our place in it will be. We look around and make judgments based on the things we see. We try to make our experiences gel with what we've been told. And in between all of this we spend very little time believing anything at all.

We are creatures of habit. We brush our teeth, go to work, eat supper, watch TV. None of these actions requires much in the way of a belief system. They require only the ability to go through the motions, to survive.

When we ask people to change their "beliefs," we are really asking them to change their habits. This is hard. While I may believe that jogging three miles a day is good for me and is what I should do, I find it hard to make this a habit. Jogging hurts, and worse, in this country, people stare at you if you run on the sidewalk. They look at you like you're nuts. They look at you like you're nuts when you go to church, too. Being looked at like you're nuts, while a daily experience for some of us, is scary for most people.

THIS IS THE difficult thing about evangelism. It isn't always clear what we're attempting to do. When we say we want to bring people to Jesus, what do we mean exactly? That we want them to say they believe in Jesus? That we want them to be baptized, join the church, and warm a pew along with the rest of us? When we share our beliefs with others, what do we expect? Bear in mind that for some people hearing about how God worked in your life last week might sound just as ridiculous as if you said a white hand reached out of a pond and tied your shoes for you. It doesn't matter how you say it: if your religious beliefs are deeply at odds with what one of your friends has seen, experienced, and been told, you have an uphill battle.

I'm not convinced you can "persuade" anyone into belief. It's more of a gut thing. If you've ever had the pleasure of attending a time-share pitch, you'll know what I mean. They'll give you a lot of evidence about why you need a time-share, and it all sounds pretty good, like you wouldn't want to argue or anything, but at the same time, you don't want a time-share. You're not a time-share kind of girl. They can flick through as many glossy magazines as they want. They can work mathematic formulas on a flip chart. They can go ahead and have all the answers. After a while your eyes glaze over, and you start to think that not only are you not buying a time-share, but from now on you'll be throwing eggs at them.

If belief is mostly a gut thing, then there is some truth to the idea that we will find it easier to accept the beliefs of people who are like us. I think that's what Paul meant when he talked about being a Jew or a Greek or a slave, etc., depending on whom he was with. It's a simple exercise of the imagination—putting yourself in another's shoes. Recognizing that if you had his character and life experiences, you would probably behave and think the way he does.

There are still no guarantees. There may be nothing you can do, no amount of relevance or kindness you can muster, that will convince your friends to become Christians. This is why I'm not 100 percent sold on the idea of friendship evangelism. I prefer plain old friendship. We ought to be interested in people because we're people too, not because we're trying to sell them, you know, a time-share.

If we're not really interested in people, then we shouldn't pretend that we are. Instead, maybe we should think about why that is.

Are you afraid to get close to other people because you'll have to reveal that you don't understand some aspects of what you believe? I wouldn't worry about it. Belief is a strange, messy thing. When you express it, you're trying to take the whole world and cram it into a few mouthfuls of words. The most important experiences are the ones that leave you speechless anyway. Go ahead and embrace the uncertainty, the silence, the invisible, the miraculous—all the things you know but could never in a lifetime prove. And try to express them. As unlikely as it may seem, you may find others who have seen just what you have. Maybe your experience isn't so weird. Someone may say, "No way! I saw a hand just like that too!"

If anyone ever says this to me, I will almost certainly shun that individual. I have enough problems without dealing with whacked-out friends.

DEAD OR ALIVE

I KNOW THIS guy who I'll call John because I get the feeling he doesn't care too much for Jack. One day, back when I had a job and we both worked in the same building, I wandered into his office and happened to see a book called *In Search of Schrödinger's Cat*.

"Schrödinger had a cat?" I said. "That little guy from *Peanuts*, with the piano? He's my favorite. No, Charlie Brown is. No, I take that back. It's Snoopy. But Schrödinger's my second favorite. I love that little piano. What happened to the cat?"

"American education," John said, shaking his head. "Didn't they teach you any science?"

"A mole is a mole is a mole is a mole," I said. "But here's a philosophical question for you, Jack: do you think it's possible that sometimes a mole is really a gerbil? Go ahead. Chew it over."

"Did you sniff a lot of glue back in your rebellious teenage years?"

"What do you mean by 'a lot'?"

AWHILE BACK I was having one of my biweekly nihilistic meltdowns. What's the point of it all? My life is meaningless. Everything is meaningless. Why shouldn't I throw myself off a bridge? (I am both moody and melodramatic. I believe the precise psychological term is Big Grumpy Baby.) The woman I'd chosen to dump on is older than I am, and I admire her. She is one of those rare older people who is actually wise. When I grow up—well, yes, the universe will burst into spontaneous applause—I want to be a combination of her and Helen Mirren from *Prime Suspect*. The woman rolled her eyes ever so slightly, kicked her feet up on her desk, and said, "Batman [this is the term of endearment all my nearest and dearest friends use when addressing me], the purpose of your life is to become—as fully as you can— the person you were created to be."

Whoa! Pretty good, huh? This satisfied me for a few days, until I suddenly thought, *But wait a minute—how am I supposed to know what kind of person I was created to be? And what if becoming that person is too hard?*

I have a feeling I know the answers my wise friend would give: (a) finding out is part of the journey, and (b) tough.

ERWIN RUDOLF JOSEF Alexander Schrödinger (1887-1961) was a Nobel Prize-winning Austrian physicist. His "cat" is actually an illustration devised to explain Heisenberg's uncertainty principle—also known as the observer's paradox or quantum indeterminacy.

"Go ahead," John said, "Borrow the book. Supplement your scanty and shameful education."

You put a cat (theoretically—that means "not really") in a steel chamber along with a vial of hydrocyanic acid. The chamber also contains a very small amount of a radioactive substance. If even a single atom of the substance decays, a device trips a hammer that breaks the vial, releasing the poison and killing the cat. The observer cannot know at any given time whether or not an atom of the substance has decayed, and therefore, he cannot know whether the cat is dead or alive. Since we can't know, the cat is in a state of superposition—both dead and alive, according to quantum law—until someone observes it. Observation itself affects the outcome.

Since I'm incapable of thinking about anything containing the words "quantum" or "physics" for more than about 10 seconds without risking massive head explosion, we're now leaving Nobel land and entering my world, where everything is purple and green and always spinning.

When I hear this illustration, I think, *Poor kitty.* And then, at the risk of revealing the bottomless depths of my pathological narcissism, I have to confess that the next thing I think is *Poor me.*

Only within the past few years did I begin to really notice the passage of time and to realize what this meant for me. My 5-year-old son composed a little jingle just this evening, and I think it sums, well, everything up rather well. I can see him writing for Hallmark someday:

First you're a baby/Then you're a child/Then you grow up/And then you die.

"Do you like it?" he squealed, laughing and bouncing up and down on my stomach.

"It's very accurate," I said, bursting into tears. People have a variety of phobias. Some are afraid of peanut butter getting stuck to the roof of their mouths *(Arachibutyrophobia)* or flutes *(Aulophobia)* or the Northern Lights *(Auroraphobia)*, but I'm not that interesting. I suffer from your garden-variety death phobia.

In theory, there are some benefits to getting older and, in particular, to recognizing that your life—at least the present one—will not go on forever. If you're wise, you start making observations. You take measurements (though not so much of your waist). If you're brave enough to look at your life once in a while, both the act of observation and the reality of what you see can make profound differences in your future choices.

The thing is, it's a lot easier to simply plod on, so that's what most of us do. Taking stock, changing direction—these things get harder as your muscles get softer. Measuring your life, thinking about whether you're becoming the person you want to be, pondering whether there'll be anything worth etching on your tombstone—well, these are all morbid thoughts, yes, but they're also scary for a whole lot of other reasons.

What if you find that changes need to be made in your life? What if, in order to live as full a life as you can imagine, you have to do something that terrifies you? What if you make the wrong move? What if you become—heaven forbid—the architect of your own misery? What if—in a cruel twist of fate—all those people who warned you against pipe dreams and who urged you to be sensible turn out to be right? What if they come to visit when you're living in a box, wearing two pairs of trousers, and, in a phrase made famous by Job's friends, say, "Told you so"? What if, upon leaving, they hand you a sweaty coin out of pity and tell you not to spend it on alcohol?

Do you ever feel like that cat—simultaneously dead and alive? Do you move from one pointless task to the next in a kind of fog and no matter how many times you blink and how much coffee you guzzle, you can't ever quite wake up? The list of things you are afraid of is long. You have a pulse and are technically "alive," but you're also simultaneously kinda dead—or, to coin a whole new term: hypo-alive.

What needs to happen to make you fully alive? Instead of "hoping for the best," what are you doing to ensure that your life is moving in a positive direction?

AT THE AGE of 24, while completing the final requirements for my master's degree in education, I realized I hated teaching secondary school. Hated marking pornographic sketches of Romeo and Juliet, hated being alternately threatened and sexually harassed by 12-year-olds, and hated the sound of my own shrill voice bouncing off the construction-papered walls of classrooms decorated with the illiterate work of kids who will learn history only when it's "the gory bits" and who like assignments only when they involve felt-tip markers and the command to "color in." The fact that these students are very much like me does not, I'm afraid, elicit much (any?) of my sympathy.

I have a terrible fear of quitting. My people, the ones who lived in tents and ate muskrats and felled trees and were sometimes felled by trees, never thought about whether they liked anything. They didn't worry about whether they were fulfilled. They got up and got going. There is enough of this still left in me that I feel guilty for wondering whether there might be more to life than a life I hate.

When I think of quitting anything, I imagine the universe, you know, *imploding*. This is how you gauge whether your actions are courageous—what you believe their consequences to be. Contravening taboos, while the most frightening of actions, is also by far the most liberating.

I don't quit things very often, but every time I do, I feel reborn. Quitting one thing is the beginning of everything else. It is the ultimate statement of independence. And when I quit teaching, contrary to my expectations, I didn't feel like a quitter. I rode my bicycle home triumphant. I had never felt better in my life. Free. It's the kind of freedom you feel only when you've made a choice (usually a choice that might be incredibly stupid) that involves throwing away years of hard work, a decision that no one in full possession of his or her faculties would urge you to make—but one that feels oh-so-right-it-can't-be-wrong.

If you want to live, not a hypo-life, not a half-life, not a life in superposition, but a real life—you have to be prepared to quit. Quit habits that are dragging you down, quit toxic friendships, quit wasting time fulfilling other people's expectations, and quit waiting for something miraculous to kick you off your seat. Also, you have to quit being such a chicken.

My mother told me once, "Don't be afraid of life." Someday I would like to understand what that means. That and "quantum." And also "cat."

A FRIEND TOLD me that her dream is to live in a castle and paint.

"What d'ya need the castle for?" I asked. "Why not paint where you are?"

"I'm afraid I might not be good at it," she said. "What if it turns out I can't paint? Then I won't have this dream to think about anymore."

Thumbs down on the sentiment, but two thumbs up to this woman not only for knowing the truth but for having the guts to say it. People are so rarely honest. I would expect most people to tell me how they're planning to start painting "real soon" when things "calm down a bit." What we don't like to say is that we chose hypo-life because it's less scary, less risky. It hurts somewhat less.

Out of all the people I know, very few of them are doing the thing they would do or becoming the person they would be if they had all the choices in the world. Why? Because they're waiting for something. What?

I hate being all didactic, but I've thus far rambled in such an insane way that I fear you may miss the point. Normally that wouldn't bother me at all (I'm not big on points), but this one is actually important.

I want you to envision a neon sign. Right now it's dark, but here I go: I'm reaching for the electric switch. Put on your sunglasses—this sucker's bright. It's also graced with the truly illiterate question mark flanked by two exclamation points for "extra" emphasis. Hang this neon sign in your peripheral vision where it will irritate you like those automatic multicolored blinking Christmas tree lights. I hope it ruins your days and haunts your sleep and causes you to run toward whatever you've been running from. Here goes: "You! Bozo! What are you waiting for!?!"

CAN YOU FEEL THE LOVE?

"FOR SEPTEMBER I want you to write an article on leadership," said this youth magazine editor (with whom I share a house, two kids, and sometimes a toothbrush). "It's for the Spain Youth Leadership Convention." Then he poked me. "Did you hear what I said? *Leadership.*"

"Wha?" I said, rubbing my eyes. All I heard was the last word, *leadership.* The rest, I've intuited.

It was 2:00 a.m. That's 2:00 in the morning for those of you unaccustomed to the metric system.

"I'm sleeping," I muttered.

"Sorry. So you think you can write on leadership?"

"Honey, I can write on twice-used toilet paper thrown up a creek without a paddle."

"What's that mean?"

"It means I'm sleeping. Stop talking. Don't even think about snoring. Get your feet off me."

A few minutes later he was snoring, and I was lying awake in the dark, eyes open wide in fear and perplexity. "Lea-der-ship," I mused, pronouncing the syllables carefully, heart palpitating. "Sounds familiar. What is that? Like some kind of fish?"

I AM TOTALLY the kind of person who would wear an "I Heart Anarchy" T-shirt. I don't like the idea of being led. Nothing makes me more furious than being told—by some leader or another—what I'm supposed to be all excited about. "It's the year of the woman, people! It's the year of the kangaroo! It's the year of the kangaroo woman! Let's get excited."

"Year of the what?" I'll rage until everyone is sick of me. "Baby, I *am* a woman. Every year is year of the woman around here. And don't even get me started on marsupials."

But the curse of my generation is that while we've been disappointed too often and too spectacularly to escape a certain (high) degree of cynicism about our leaders, we're also idealistic and want to follow somebody great. I don't want anybody telling me what to do, but I do want someone to inspire me, to give me hope, to make me believe that people faced with difficult decisions will do the right thing, that the world can be better than it is. That I can be better than I am. That someone will do something about, oh, I don't know, hoodies. (During the time I lived in the U.K., some government officials were proposing a law preventing young people from wearing hooded sweatshirts in the U.K.'s largest shopping mall. They'll probably ban balaclavas next. Grumble. They come in so handy on those bad-hair/bad-face/fat-neck days.)

I'm also the kind of person who would suddenly, out of nowhere, say, "Why don't we ever do year of the kangaroo anymore? That was awesome!"

THE NEXT MORNING I had the dictionary cracked open to L while I drank my morning coffee. I'm telling you, there are some great words on page 1046 of the *New Oxford Dictionary*. Here's an example that doesn't even involve veering dangerously off my narrow, dominant theme: *leaderene*. That's "a female leader, especially an autocratic one," and it originated as a "humorous" name for Margaret Thatcher in the 1980s. H'mm. That's a thinker.

The editor joined me on the deck, but not before I snapped the dictionary shut, threw it over the fence, and acted as if I'd been drinking coffee and pondering the wonders of the natural world.

"So, leadership," he said.

"You mean 'the action of leading a group of people or an organization'? 'the state or position of being a leader'? Why, yes. I've already developed some groundbreaking thoughts."

"Look," he said. "I trust you and all, but just don't say anything too risqué. None of that about how you love Fidel Castro and want to be a dictator or how you think Tony Blair is sexy. That's just gross and weird. OK?" That pretty much wiped out my whole first page.

I hid my disappointment. I gave him the wink and the gun, aiming my index finger like the barrel of a pistol and pulling the trigger with my thumb. "Gotcha," I said. "Trust me. I'm on top of it. And already bludgeoning it with a heavy brick. Figuratively speaking."

"ASSIGNED WRITING," I muttered for weeks. "This stinks."

But I went ahead and struck up a few random conversations on the subject, hoping someone would say something I could use. Something true. Or stupid. I ain't fussy.

"You know what I love?" one man in a Greek fisherman's cap said. "I love when you see these guys—you know, the ones who are so desperate to be in charge—putting themselves forward. I love how the Lord just sweeps down like thunder and puts them in their place."

"How does He do that?" I asked, genuinely intrigued.

"He has His ways," the man said, nodding ominously. "He has a thousand ways."

"So you're saying one shouldn't seek leadership?"

"Seek and ye shall find."

"Find what?"

"The pearl of great price."

"What pearl?"

"The pearl for which many go knocking, but few find."

"Dude," I said. "You're blowing my mind. But can I just say—don't get mad—that thunder doesn't 'sweep down'? Hey, have you ever heard of a 'leaderene'?"

I thought, since he was English, that the word alone would send him into spasms of laughter. But he just frowned, scratched his head, and said, "I've heard of a Nazarene."

LUCKY FOR ME, I recently took my son to *The Lion King* at the Lyceum Theatre in London.

Now, the folks at Disney know a thing or three about leadership. The three central characters—Mufasa, Scar, and Simba—each embody a certain type of leader.

Mufasa is king. He accepts this role gladly—not for the power it gives him, but because it enables him to fulfill his place in the "circle of life." He knows that a leader is first a servant. He is part of a long line of kings, looking to the past to help him fulfill his role.

Scar, the king's younger brother, is heir to the throne—until Simba is born. Scar is bitter because he isn't in charge and never will be. He doesn't realize that leadership isn't so much a perk as a privilege. He spends his time plotting against the king and making snide remarks. When he finally kills

Mufasa, chases Simba from the area, and assumes the throne, he is, of course, a horrible king. The lions are soon starving in a horrid hyena-infested wasteland. Scar thinks leadership is about wearing a crown and telling others what to do. In the cartoon version—and this is significant—he alone, played by Jeremy Irons, speaks with a British accent. In grand movie tradition, that's how you know he's cold, brilliant, evil, and phony.

Simba doesn't, at first, have the strength to fight for the throne. Fear and guilt drive him to adopt the philosophy "hakuna matata"—"no worries." He has to discover who he is and why it is so important that he become the leader he was meant to be. In maturity he will be very much the great leader Mufasa was. But he has to go back and fight for it.

He has to put himself forward. He has to openly admit wanting leadership. He has to risk being pegged as one of those people who are "so desperate to be in charge."

Even though I'd already seen the cartoon version, I sat with fists clenched, hoping Simba would persuade Nala to join him in his carefree, happy life. "Don't go back!" I shouted, prompting dark looks from my fellow theater patrons. "Run free, Simba! You can feel the love anywhere!"

The story ends with Simba defeating Scar and taking his throne. What it doesn't show is how, after approximately two days of much rejoicing, the pride of lions begin to grumble and give Simba a hard time. They want to go back to Egypt. Their lives were better in the brick manufacturing plant. They're sick of manna and want quail. They build a golden calf and worship it. Simba's soon feeling no love, probably wondering why he came back.

The real question is "Why would anyone want to be a leader?"

There is simply no explanation as to why a person with both a healthy psyche and any other option—Burger King, Little Chef—would willingly take a job that causes people to, on a good day, draw unflattering cartoons of them and, on a bad day, fire at them from a book depository window.

And if you think that sounds dangerous, just try being chair of the church floral committee.

Yet people take these positions. People—I'm reasonably sure they're human—come out of the safety of their own homes and offer their talents, gladly stepping into the line of fire, arms raised in surrender, hoping they'll get a chance to speak before someone takes them out.

"Simba *has* to go back," my son whispered at the theater. "If he doesn't, the lions will starve."

"So?" I said.

"Mama! You can't just let your friends starve or be eaten by hyenas."

No, I don't suppose you can—but people do just that every day. That's why we need leaders: those who feel, quite keenly, a sense of personal responsibility.

WHEN I WAS a teen, the conference president seemed rather frightening. He'd breeze into school or summer camp with his entourage to see whether we met with his approval. Teachers threatened us with death by dismemberment if we misbehaved. I thought he was a creep.

"What a phony," I'd say. "He just shows up to get his picture taken."

Later my parents became friends with the man, and they told me something interesting about him. The conference president was, as they put it, "a major Mickey Mouse nut." He had a huge collection of Mickey Mouse memorabilia—hundreds of items.

I didn't quite know what to do with a grown man who collected Mickey Mouse memorabilia. I didn't know if I wanted to kick him or give him a big hug, but that little snippet made this man real. A man with a silly hobby isn't intimidating. Sometimes leaders feel pressure to appear dignified and perfect, but maybe the best-kept secret in the world is that they *shouldn't*. I'm not saying anyone will respect or follow a man who collects Strawberry Shortcake figurines, but, well, I probably would.

IN 1999 THE World Trade Organization (WTO) held its meeting in Seattle. Fidel Castro was invited to attend, and while he was unable to make it, many people were pretty excited by the possibility of his visit. Castro has a certain cult status. In part, it's because the Old White Guys With the Side Partings don't like him, and the rest of us are perverse enough to think, *If they hate him, he's my new best friend!*

It also has to be the WYSIWYG (What You See Is What You Get) factor. He looks like what he is—an old sixties radical with an unkempt beard, usually photographed in military fatigues, though I've seen a couple of rather disturbing photos of him looking like a city councilman in a dark suit with the ubiquitous, and always alarming, red tie. Otherwise, he seems authentic, and in a world full of people deliberately trying to jumble their messages beyond recognition, it is refreshing to see someone real, even if "real" means "dictator."

So what's my point? If you want to lead—in the free world—someone has to follow you. And to have followers, you must give them a reason to tag along for the ride.

Contrast Castro's convincing workers-of-the-world-unite air with the strange and almost schizophrenic behavior of U.S. presidential candidate Al Gore in 2000. Clearly worried that he was perceived as "boring," Mr. Gore went to great lengths to appear alternately cool, groovy, exciting, impassioned, and, apparently, as if suffering from some sort of head trauma. It was deeply creepy for many people that a man in his late 40s should have so little idea of who he is. Gore should have easily won, but he lost the election by a thin margin—and many of us still cry our eyes out every night as a result. Certainly his lack of authenticity was a deciding factor. A man who is inauthentic is not trustworthy. What is he hiding?

Authenticity doesn't make you a good leader. You could easily be an authentic cannibal. Castro is as popular among youngish Americans as lower-back tattoos. And let's face it, Cuban-Americans hate him. The people crossing the water in makeshift boats, sprinting for the Florida beach before INS officials can stop them, don't appear to be overly enthralled with life in Castro's Cuba.

Lack of authenticity, however, does absolutely make you a bad leader. Why? Because your job is to inspire people, not give them the heebie-jeebies. You want them to hear what you're saying, not wonder, "Why don't his eyes smile when his lips do? Why does she keep using words that don't flow naturally from her mouth? Why does he look as though his red tie is strangling him?"

If you're crazy enough, or compelled enough, to want to be a leader, first you have to find your voice. You need to have something to say that's worth saying. You have to be real. Say what you think. Do what you say. If you have a Mickey Mouse collection, tell people. They'll like you better for it. Don't lie. Don't use and abuse people. Don't wear a red tie.

If people are going to hate you—and if you're a leader, some of them will—you should at least allow them to hate the real you. Maybe they'll call you a leaderene or something even more "humorous." You'll live. I even envy you. It has always been my wish to be referred to as "the Iron Lady," but instead, people keep calling me "that loser in the hoodie."

And this may interest you: I popped open the dictionary and had another look. "Leaderene" is a play on *all those* female names that end in "ene," like Marlene. And Darlene. *Now* I get it. Oh, the Brits and their "sense of humor." I literally can't stop laughing.

MAROC IN THE CORNER

IN THE SUMMER of 2005 an American visitor and I were discussing the London terrorist bombings with an English person. "I wish they'd just bomb the Americans some more and leave us alone," he said.

I smiled, and I imagine he figured I found his remark amusing. Really, I wasn't so much smiling as baring my teeth. Baring my teeth and flinching. Flinching and mentally composing the first few paragraphs of this article.

If I didn't write, I'd probably shout and throw things . . . well, more often than I currently do.

"Count to 10," I whispered. "Naw. Better make it 1,000."

AS A KID I was obsessed with what I would have called "foreigners"— namely, people who are not from North America. I'd sit in hotel rooms and study the local dialects from the Gideon Bible tucked inside the bedside table. I'd pore over maps and encyclopedias, memorizing details about the various peoples of the world—what they wear, what they eat, whether or not they are offended by feet or by the "OK" gesture.

I came to England to study at a multinational college when I was 21. My goal was to make all these great friends from different countries. I figured that I'd find out about the world—all the things I'd always wanted to know.

On my first day I attended a "sensitivity" meeting for American students only. The purpose of the meeting was to teach us all the myriad ways in which our behavior, speech, attitudes, points of view, and life experiences were "offensive" to Europeans and should be suppressed or altered if possible.

"Europeans see Americans as silly and childlike," the expatriate professor explained. "If you want people to take you seriously, you need to act more European."

We couldn't talk too loud or laugh too much or be boisterous. We shouldn't call things quaint. We shouldn't talk about what things are like at home.

"Try not to talk at all," the professor said. "But if you have to, here's a tip: they hate it when you pronounce things wrong. You say it 'Tems,' not 'Thaymes.' You call it 'Lester,' not 'Lye-ses-ter.'"

What's this? I wondered. *Can't I just be myself? Can't I learn from my mistakes? Ask questions?*

"Europeans don't like it when you ask lots of questions," the professor continued. "If you want people to like you," he cautioned, "just *don't* be yourselves."

The dozens of friends I'd imagined didn't really materialize. "Americans are stupid," the other students would lecture, waving their arms around. "Americans don't know the difference between Sweden and Switzerland."

As an individual who has—on more than one occasion—stuck her finger in a live socket, I won't bother to argue against the charge of stupidity when applied to me. I feel sorry for those poor guys at NASA, though. And also Bill Gates. Why should they be tainted along with the rest of us?

It used to make me really angry. Angry and also startled at the level of animosity directed at me, just a girl from Washington State. Not a character from *Dynasty* or *Dallas,* not a political figure—just a girl in old Doc Martens and a flannel shirt who had always wanted to know what the world was like.

"What is wrong with these people?" I'd rage. But what I really meant, what I secretly worried, is "What is wrong with me?"

(For the record, I like being silly and childlike. I like to marvel at things. I enjoy laughing until I snort. It is not imperative that anyone take me seriously.)

IN THE EARLY hours of the morning on an overnight train from Bari to Rome, my friend and I were roused from a deep sleep by a small, mustached, and extremely agitated Italian man. He'd come into our train compartment to check our tickets and couldn't wake us. When he finally shouted and shook us awake, we had eye-popping headaches.

It turned out we'd been gassed and my friend's video camera stolen. The train was searched, the camera recovered, and a man arrested—dragged off the train into the police station. The conductor treated us to sugary espresso and pastries. He shook his finger and said, "No Italian. *No Italian.*"

The thief was from somewhere in North Africa. The Italians called him a "Maroc," which I figured maybe meant Moroccan. (I hope it isn't a bad word. If it is, I hope no one reading this speaks Italian.) The police raised their arms above their heads and bowed to the floor repeatedly. The man was a Muslim.

I wore a crucifix on a chain around my neck, more as a fashion statement than a statement of faith. They pointed at their own large crucifix, hanging from the wall of the small smoky room. We couldn't speak the same language, but we had something in common.

These police officers were very kind. They gave us food, let us take showers, and offered tempting proposals of marriage. When a grizzled old man with a fat cigar had finished typing what I can only assume was an incident report, they put us on the next train to Rome and waved good-bye.

The thief, being a thief and a Maroc and a Muslim and a man, didn't fare so well. The police kept taking him away and then bringing him back, shoving him down in the corner where he sat, shackled and staring at the floor. I worried that they were roughing him up in a back alley somewhere. They'd pull their guns from their holsters (attached with what appeared to be curly telephone cords) and point them in his face and shout. Once they held him, arms cuffed behind his back, and indicated that we could punch him. Sock him in the stomach, in the face, below the belt.

Instead, we filmed him with the video camera he stole. I narrated— something along the lines of "Look at this jerk who gassed us and stole our camera." I haven't watched the tape in years. Instead, I rely on the one in my head. It didn't occur to me then—I was too young and hadn't really learned how it feels to be different. But now, when I remember the man shackled on the floor with downcast eyes and a crowd of natives mocking him and all the things that were important to him, I think, *Buddy, in another life you and I could have almost been friends.*

"DO YOU UNDERSTAND what the phrase 'At the end of the day' means?" someone asked me a few years ago.

"Dude," I said. "I speak English."

"No, you speak American."

"OK." (Never argue with an imbecile.)

"Use it in a sentence."

"All right. At the end of the day, no matter what else happens, I will still be American. And at the end of the day, if I pass this test, you'll devise another one to exclude me. At the end of the day, I'm not sure I care."

Of course I didn't say any of this out loud. This is only what I thought.

66

Out loud, I formed a sentence. I don't remember whether the man was impressed. If he was, he shouldn't have been. Like I said, I speak English. English *and* American. Tomato, tomato.

But just so we're clear, I consider all the years I've felt sort of patronized, mocked, and isolated—what you could almost call my time in the corner—to be the best and most valuable experience of my life so far. The view from the corner is not one you get from any other part of the room. I am, after all, the girl who wanted to know about the world. This is the only way. Little by little, I'm excavating. I'm brushing away the dirt slowly, carefully. Shapes emerge.

MY FIRST FEW years of life as a permanent British resident—and in total, I did 12 years—were disorienting. It wasn't so much that I was in a different place as it was that I felt like a different person. There were all these echoes of all the things I wasn't supposed to be. Pile up enough don'ts, and there isn't much left to do. I felt paralyzed and demonstrated little personality. I was afraid it would be the wrong kind, that people would roll their eyes in my direction. There were times I felt I couldn't breathe.

Time, however, as everyone knows, does its thing, and after a while I began to feel myself rising to the surface again, slowly, slowly, toward the light, finally bursting through with a great gasp for air. I'm alive. I'm still alive, and I'm still me.

Me, but different. Not precisely the girl in the Doc Martens who thought anywhere would be more interesting than home. More the girl who knows that home can be anywhere you survive long enough that you forget you're not really from there, and when people remind you, you shrug and figure it doesn't matter that much anyway.

MY GUEST WAS shocked by what the English person said. "They want us to be bombed?" he asked later. "Us? Like you and me?"

It was an unusually nasty statement—most people just stick to saying we're fat and stupid, but nevertheless worthy of life. Even so, I had to think about it for a while. Lots of people do believe that almost everything wrong with the world is our fault. "I don't think so," I said finally. "He's probably just talking."

People shoot off their mouths. They say things that are alternately stupid, hurtful, callous, or just plain wrong. I do it. We all do it. We should probably stop ripping each other apart, but we probably won't. What are you gonna do? Get mad? Doesn't help. Bite back? Futile. Dig a hole and climb in? Sad. Pathetic.

Some of you, like me, will have been criticized or stereotyped because of your race or nationality or religion or sex. In a way, we can count ourselves lucky. When people are busy negatively characterizing you because of your group affiliation, they have less time to pick out what's really wrong with you.

Others face devastating criticism because of other characteristics they can't—and maybe shouldn't—change, but that others feel obliged to point out. Maybe you are trying to make a real difference in your community, and people are threatened at the prospect of change. You will feel discouraged and be tempted to give up. Don't.

Lots of times I thought it would be easier to go back to the United States, and when I finally did, it was easier in some ways, but it was still just life. There are some things I like. I don't have to spend so much time explaining myself. People don't hear my accent and chase me into the Tube or anywhere else, screaming that they are going to kill me. But that happened only once in London, and it was a long time ago. As a character on that TV show *Ally McBeal* would say: "Bygones."

I would feel like a failure if I hadn't stuck around long enough for the "foreign" experience to change me enough to make it worthwhile. When I made the decision to return back to the U.S., I walked with slow, purposeful steps, not running with the chaotic gait of the frenzied and frightened. No matter which direction you go in life, remember that rule from primary school: walk, don't run.

People will tell you that criticisms and mockery say more about your tormenters than they do about you. This is true, but not necessarily helpful— just as someone repeatedly chanting "It's not real" during a horror movie doesn't necessarily keep you from screaming when the monster pops out from behind the door. You feel what you feel.

The only advice I can give is the same thing I'd tell any woman about to deliver a baby. Just breathe. Sooner or later it will be over, and you'll have something. That something will be your self-respect. Breathe. And keep breathing. Breathe some more. At the end of the day, this is productive pain. Breathe.

PYROMANIAC'S GUIDE TO THE UNIVERSE

THE DAY I graduated from high school everyone was crying and hugging. I might have hugged one or two people (for show), but I didn't shed a tear.

"We're never going to see most of these people ever again," one girl, whom I barely knew, wailed.

"I know!" I answered brightly. "This is the best day of my life!"

She wiped her eyes. "You're funny," she said, and I could tell that by "funny" she meant "weird."

After the ceremony I stepped outside the gym, which resembled a large airplane hangar. Since we weren't, for "insurance reasons," allowed to throw our caps in celebration, there was nothing much to do. I wandered over to the white-pillared girls' dormitory that had been my home for about nine months. I wound my arm around one of the pillars, stroking it like you might a cat. I leaned in close, resting my cheek on the cool plaster and softly, menacingly, whispered a line that I'm pretty sure the Terminator stole from me:

"I'll be back."

The pillar, it seems, knew my voice; it recognized my touch.

I swear it shuddered.

FAST-FORWARD MANY a moon to last autumn. My mom phoned to say that the girls' dormitory had burned to the ground. "It's OK," she said. "No one was hurt." All the same, when I got off the phone I wept.

I didn't cry, as some might, from nostalgia, because of all the rockin' good times I'd had in that dorm. The most fun I recall having in boarding school was squirting canned "cheez" directly into my mouth while reading a tattered, orange-covered novel called *The Holocaust* and sobbing until my eyes resembled swollen, split gooseberries.

Michelle—the girl who wasn't my roommate but spent most nights crashed out on my floor and who is the reason that I still won't sleep with my arm dangling over the edge of a bed—would drop in between classes.

"You won't believe what the Nazis have done now," I'd choke.

"Worse than murdering millions of people like 50 years ago?" she'd say. Michelle is now an ER nurse in one of the gunshot capitals of the U.S. She hasn't so much as a sentimental cell in her whole biochemical makeup. I, on the other hand, cry at everything, even the ending of *Jurassic Park III.* Faced with a really sad story, I can easily sit in my pajamas for weeks.

"They broke the artist's hands," I wailed. "He can never paint again! Why would they do that? It's like killing a mockingbird. I hate the world and everything in it. Can you get me some more cheez?"

I saw Michelle just a few months ago, and while she agrees that boarding school was grim, she also claims we actually had fun—at least once. There was something that "had us in stitches" for "a couple of days."

"Something about a bran muffin," she said. "It was hilarious. Help me out: it was right after your boyfriend got kicked out of school and you had to go to the junior/senior banquet alone and everyone thought you were pathetic and you were so stressed you tanked your college entrance exams. Remember? Then we had to scrub all the bathrooms with a toothbrush dipped in bleach because we missed so many worships and they weren't going to let us take our Spanish final exam. Breathing the bleach mixed with mold made you throw up chunks of carrot in the hallway until your eyes almost popped out. That psycho from British Columbia stole my favorite T-shirt and gave it to the weird guy who we all thought was possessed. Well, I saw the weird guy a couple years ago. He works for the IRS—so it looks like we were right. Ha! Anyway, it was that same week they were drug-testing everyone and people were drinking vinegar and there was a rumor flying around that the lead singer from Guns N' Roses had died, and people were crying and screaming and arranging floral tributes made from dandelions they picked by the flagpole. Ring any bells?"

I stared at her, incredulous. "No way," I said. "I took *Spanish?*"

"WHAT ARE YOU crying about?" my husband asked, exasperated. "You hated living in the dorm."

"You don't understand me *at all!*" I wailed. "I wanted to burn it down myself! I'm a failure."

They used to do realistic drills with smoke simulators so we'd be prepared in the event of a real fire. I'd be on my belly, crawling on my elbows like a wounded soldier in the jungles of Vietnam, heading for the fire exit, all the while whispering, "Let it be real. Let it be real." If only a miracle happened and the dorm burned down, I could go home and be happy!

After every false-alarm fire drill, I'd stomp to breakfast at 6:30 the next morning in a foul mood.

"Why?" I'd rage at my friends. "Just this one little thing. That's all I want. Why can't I have it? See, this is why I don't pray. This is why I'm not religious. God doesn't care about me. He won't even do one little thing I want, like burn the dorm down. How hard is that?"

Once, after I'd vented, I raised my mug of hot chocolate to my lips to take a swig. My friend Dan stopped me. "I put salt in that," he said.

"Don't care," I answered.

"No, don't!" he shouted, pulling at my arm and causing me to slop hot chocolate all over my hot-pink stirrup pants. "I put a toenail in it. And a scab from my elbow."

I stood up, dripping hot chocolate, and shook my fist at the ceiling. "I need a bolt of lightning!" I screamed. "Right NOW!"

I waited. Obviously nothing happened.

"You and the possessed guy would make a cute couple," Dan said. "What with the way your head is spinning around."

"THAT'S HOW I'LL know I'm successful," I told the bemused woman who interviewed me for a university place. "When I have enough money that I can buy this place and burn it to the ground."

"What if they won't sell?"

I raised an eyebrow. "I'll make them an offer they can't refuse," I said in a strangled voice—my version of Marlon Brando.

The woman looked confused. She hadn't seen *The Godfather*. "What?"

"You know. Like a severed horse's head in the bed? That kind of thing? Only it would be something else. I love horses. Not too keen on wiener dogs, though. And I hate earwigs! How about that? A bed full of earwigs! Now, there's an offer you can't refuse!"

"Young lady!" the interviewer said, exhaling sharply. "I don't know whether to admit you to college or have you incarcerated."

"Depends on how desperate you are for students," I said.

INSTEAD OF MAKING even the most meager of efforts to enjoy my boarding school experience, I spent most of my spare time fantasizing about—I can't stress this enough—legal arson.

I'd lie in bed, with the shadow of my inflatable *T. rex* looming large against the wall, listening to the dreary elevator music they'd play at bedtime to calm us down, and I'd envision myself arriving—in slow motion—at the school in a long crocodile-skin trench coat and dark shades. The area would be cordoned off with yellow "Do not cross this line" tape and a team of attractive firemen making sure everything proceeded safely. I'd sit on the hood of my yellow Lamborghini—a safe distance from the school, but still within good viewing range—and detonate the buildings with a remote-control device—shattering windows and bursting the drywall into tall, leaping orange flames.

"Not one brick would be on top of another brick," I sobbed to my husband. "It was going to be wicked!"

"See, this," he said, "this is the sort of thing you should have mentioned before we got married."

"I'm sorry," I said. I wiped my eyes and took a deep breath. "I need to think more positively. Focus. Glass half full. OK. Maybe I should be grateful for the fire. I mean, just think: I might have never been rich enough to buy the dorm, and then I could have actually died with it still standing. Now, *that* would be depressing."

My husband gave me a look that seemed vaguely reminiscent. Then I realized it was exactly the way Mr. Rochester looked at his loony wife locked in the attic in *Jane Eyre*—a mixture of two parts disgust, one part pity. I'm not a marriage counselor or a talk show host or anything, but I'm pretty sure that isn't a good sign.

"Do you have any idea how insane that sounds?"

"Like on a scale from one to 10?"

"It's the most insane thing I've ever heard. And I'm a *pastor*. Explain to me: why is it essential that anything has to burn?"

What kind of mind-bending question is that? Life partners are annoying that way. They're always forcing you to explain yourself. "Why are you always leaving the cap off the toothpaste?" they ask, as if, being in too much of a hurry to replace the cap, you now happen to have a spare 10 minutes to explain why.

"You wouldn't understand," I said dismissively. "You don't have my highly sensitive temperament. Also, you never went to boarding school. Or had to *eat stew*. You didn't have a perky person in a Polo shirt come into your room every day and give you marks out of 10 for how clean your sink was. Do you have any idea what that does to the human psyche?"

"I'm beginning to see," he murmured.

WHY DOES ANYTHING have to burn? An even better question might be: Why couldn't a relatively normal person like me (don't laugh) simply take a deep breath, smile, and enjoy being 17 years old; relish being in a unique situation that, after all, lasted only nine months (seemed like nine years), and will never be repeated again? I'm done. I'll never be that kid again. (And good riddance, some might say.) I'll never have to shout "water" when I flush the toilet to prevent the girls in the showers from getting third-degree burns. I can't think how long it's been since anyone put a scab in any type of hot drink within my possession.

You expend all this energy wanting to be out of a situation, and before you know it, you couldn't be back in if you wanted to. This is life.

When you know that time is finite, that no situation, no matter how unappealing, will last forever, doesn't it seem rather pointless to spend so much time in a froth, hating everyone and everything?

This is my rational side talking. It makes up only 2 percent of the part of my brain I use, so in terms of actual size, it's only like a nanoparticle. The irrational side, the part that can hold a grudge for eternity, that conjures up visions of leaping blue-tinged flames, that thinks *I'll show them*—this part says: "Pointless? What *is* life if not one big chance to hate everything?"

MY IMPULSE HAS always been to burn everything behind me. I am a person who hacks her way through a jungle full of thick bamboo and, once on the other side, quickly tosses a flaming, petrol-soaked rag over her shoulder, and then, without looking back, heads steely-eyed toward the next jungle—thicker, denser, bigger.

The jungle is nothing to be enjoyed or savored; it is something to be endured. It is a landscape to be crossed and conquered as quickly as possible—then laid to waste and forgotten even more quickly. No macaws are taught to tap-dance in my jungle. I have no time, and I hate the jungle. Anyway, I have to get on to the next thing.

Even though I wanted to, I never took a year out to serve as a student missionary because it would have meant I'd take five years to finish college instead of four. I wanted to grow up—presumably so I could start making all that money I'd need to buy my old school. But until I heard the dorm had burned down, I'd completely forgotten my vow to reduce the entire complex to smoking charcoal. I hadn't thought about it in years.

My behavior, you see, is not even goal-oriented. It isn't a means to an end. I'm not just a pyromaniac; I'm the flame itself, mindlessly devouring, consuming.

"Closure!" I announced to my husband in a loud voice after 20 minutes of deep thought. "It's about closure."

"OK, Oprah. Whatever."

It's not about closure. My problem stems from an unwillingness to accept a situation and make the best of it. It's the basic root of all human unhappiness, according to Blaise Pascal: the inability of a person to "remain in a room." Michelle is right: there were some good times—or there could have been if I hadn't spent my time wanting to go somewhere else, fantasizing about who I would be and what I would do when it was over. I never gave a thought to who I was and what I was doing right then. If life isn't in the moment, where is it? Reality check: when it's *over*, you're dead.

IF I COULD do it all over again, I'd be a sponge instead of a flame. Instead of consuming and fantasizing about destroying, I'd sit still and soak up. I'd pay attention. I'd ask more questions and better ones. I'd take notes—then I'd remember things for real and not have to make so much stuff up—although that would take most of the fun right out of my otherwise-routine life.

It's probably not too late for me to change—and I'm working on it. I'm seeing some progress. Just the other week I was sitting on the floor watching my baby play with wooden bricks, and I suddenly realized that I'd been sitting there for maybe 20 minutes without wanting to be anywhere else. It was a good feeling, and I wish I could summon it at will. "Maybe this is how it feels to be middle-aged," I mused. If so, it's not as dire as I had always imagined it to be.

The woman who admitted me to college looked at my form and said, "You're planning to study history."

"Uh-huh."

"So what kind of get-rich-quick job do you reckon you're going to get with a degree in history?"

She was a worthy adversary.

"Um," I said, trying to think. Job?

She flashed a wicked grin. "Yeah, I think the school's pretty safe."

Ha! Smarty-pants. Shows what she knows about the lurking dangers of a faulty boiler.

SIGN UNDER TEST

TODAY I WENT to Starbucks. While driving, I spotted a sign on the side of the road. It was one of those black digital signs that seem to pop up at random in urban areas, purporting to offer "traffic information." More frequently they are blank or contain messages that make no sense at all. This one said, "Sign under test."

"Huh?" I said out loud as I slowed down to gawk. What did it mean? A command? Was I supposed to get out of my car? Sign something (under the mysterious "test")? Was I being tested by hidden policemen? aliens? I looked up, half expecting to see a huge test looming over the sign. As is often the case in such situations, the more I thought about it, the less sense it made.

"Think less," a good friend once advised. "A lot less. Take up knitting instead. Very soothing."

MY BROTHER AND I used to walk into Bracknell from Newbold College and freak out about how we didn't know how anything worked. I most frequently experience this feeling of helplessness whenever I am required to seek "technical support." This typically takes the form of an Irish bloke on the phone using alien words like "router" for 10 minutes and then saying he can't help me.

"We are totally alienated from our environment," my brother would say. "We don't know how to survive in the world. We use cars and computers, but we don't know how they work. We can't fix them; we can't live without them."

"What about this?" he said once, gesturing to the chocolate shakes we'd picked up at Sainsbury's. "What is this stuff? We couldn't make this. I don't know what half the ingredients even are. What's guar gum? Where do you get that? If there were a nuclear explosion and I was the last person alive, I wouldn't know what to do."

This was the first time I'd ever really considered my lack of ability to survive. It was—and continues to be—profoundly depressing.

"I wish we were Bushmen of the Kalahari," I said. "Then we'd know how to do everything. We would be one with our environment. We'd know how to get water from a gourd. Also, we'd speak that really cool tongue-clicking language."

"!Kung," my brother said.

SOMETIMES I THINK that when I get around to it I'm going to compile a notebook of all the questions I should have asked. "Is that a genuine human foot?" is the question I should have asked a man on a mall bench some years ago when I saw him holding and stroking what appeared to be . . . a human foot.

If I started to record all the situations in which I feel lost and confused—signaled by an overwhelming desire to laugh—I think I'd be horrified at how frequently I haven't a clue as to what is going on around me.

I don't know how the world works. My brow is perpetually wrinkled. I don't know how to make fire or where to get clean water in the event of a breakdown of the infrastructure (whatever that is). I struggle to decipher signs. The nature and operating principles of betting agencies baffle me, and I couldn't tell you precisely what a "piston" is. Who buys all those red stuffed "love devils" that are always for sale, in the hundreds, around Valentine's Day? Why do characters on *EastEnders* finish most of their sentences with the phrase "and all"? "And all what?" I'm always shouting at the TV.

Everything often seems alien and wrong and ridiculous—as if it has nothing to do with me. "Where was I when we voted on this?" I want to yell at no one in particular. "Mr. Chair, I'd like to register my objection. This isn't the world I want. Why didn't anybody ask me? Was I in the bathroom or what?"

And I'm not even addressing events on the world stage. I'm only talking about things in the St. Albans/Watford/Hemel triangle—sometimes known colloquially as the "Triangle of Doom." Know how many planes have mysteriously gone missing around here? No? Neither do I. That fact alone should make us suspicious.

FROM HIS CAR seat my baby watched me in the rearview mirror as I raved about the sign. "Ba!" he said. "Ba, ba, BA!"

"What's that, Lassie?" I said. "You think it's the sign that's being tested? But that's impossible. Why on earth would the people—or whatever they are—who control the sign feel compelled to share that particular bit of information with me, let alone all the other motorists on this route?"

"Ba!" my baby said.

"You're right," I nodded, stroking my chin. "It must be a code. You think about it, and I'll think about it, and maybe together we can break it. The future of the world could be in our hands. Go, go, Gadget brain."

By this time I'd parked my car in a too-tight space and switched off the engine. I turned and smiled at my baby. He responded by throwing a banana peel—with much of the munched-up banana still intact—in my face.

BY NOW YOU are probably thinking, with regard to me, "What a dummy." Perfecto. This brings me—seamlessly—into my next vignette.

As I waited for the elevator in the Watford branch of Borders, I noticed an entire wall covered with those yellow "dummies" guides. Most of them were straightforward; they were what I'd expect. *PCs for Dummies. Sewing for Dummies. Personal Finance for Dummies.* Then I saw *Living With Hepatitis C for Dummies.*

"Hepatitis C?" I said in a loud, incredulous voice just as the elevator doors opened and a nice family stepped off, looked at me, and scuttled off toward the DVD section.

The bizarre, planets-in-alignment thing—and I don't think this can be just a coincidence—was that I'd been listening to the radio that very morning and a dull-voiced expert came on to warn the listening public about how there were something like a hundred million people in the U.K. who have hepatitis C and don't even know it.

"A hundred million," I muttered as I maneuvered my stroller onto the elevator. "That's like everyone in this whole country plus France! What is hepatitis C, anyway? How would a nondummy live with it? Isn't there a celebrity with some kind of hepatitis? Pamela Anderson? Or is it Pamela Lee? Is that the same person? How many kinds of hepatitis are there? Is there one for every letter of the alphabet or what? What color is the hepatitis ribbon of hope? Why is calling people 'dummies' an effective marketing tool? Isn't it kind of sick to have a dummies guide for a disease?"

Have I mentioned that "Oops, I Did It Again," by Britney Spears, was piping through the store? Or that it was only seven minutes past 9:00 in the morning and that I was still picking sleepers out of the inside corners of my eyes?

"Think less," my friend advised. Oh, baby. I would if I could.

"WHAT ARE YOU writing about?" my dad asked when I spoke to him on the phone.

"I'm not entirely sure," I said. "I think it's about how everywhere you go you're pelted with useless and annoying information. And noise. You spend your whole life trying to make sense of things that don't even matter. The only things you know about are trivia. I don't know how to make fire, Dad! And yet I do know all the words to "You're Beautiful," by Captain James Blunt. I didn't even try to learn them. I learned those lyrics almost against my will. I feel kind of violated."

"I get you," Dad said. "Take this cruise your mom and I went on this year to Alaska. They played Whitney Houston the whole time. Even this one time, we pulled up in Glacier Bay National Park, and they told us to all be quiet so we could listen to the Margerie Glacier, and guess what? Whitney Houston was still howling in the background. "I Wanna Dance With Somebody." Couldn't hear anything. Then we docked in Ketchikan, and I walked two miles to a Safeway for some tapioca pudding. What do I hear when I walk through the automatic doors? Whitney Houston."

"Messed-up story," I said. "Just think if it had been Frank Sinatra."

"Tell me about it," Dad said.

ANYMORE, IT DOESN'T take as unusual a sight as a man stroking a human foot in a shopping mall to bend my antennae. Some days everything I witness seems strange. I flatter myself that I'm going through a period of heightened awareness, but I might just as well be cracking up.

After Starbucks we went to ASDA. I don't go there very often. Too much bright-green has a negative effect on my nervous system. Also, I dislike having to insert a one-pound coin in my shopping cart. I am bothered that "they" think this acts as a deterrent to stealing the cart. My character keenly feels the crude assassination attempt. The ASDA people don't trust me—and I don't trust them.

As I wandered around, picking over hideous Halloween masks that cost—wait for it—16 pence each (half the price of a cheap loaf of bread), I became aware of a voice crackling on the store intercom. It rambled at length about cups of tea and the importance of families. Then the voice said, in as spectacular a non sequitur as I've ever heard: "Look at all the smiling faces!"

"What the hooey?" I said, looking around to see what my fellow shoppers thought of this ridiculous and bizarre speech. No one appeared to be listening. Their faces weren't smiling, either. They were too busy piling their carts with masks and plastic jack-o'-lanterns. I took out my notebook and started scribbling. "ASDA," I wrote. "11:13 a.m. 'Look at all the smiling faces.' I suspect that after years of trying, I have finally entered the Twilight Zone."

The intercom crackled again, and I almost expected a personal message telling me to work on my attitude. I see a Miss Grumpy on aisle 12. But what it said this time was even more baffling than the "Sign Under Test" sign. "Attention. We have a runner on aisle 4."

A runner? On aisle 4? Is that a guy who's just stuffed a bottle of Fairy Liquid down the front of his gray sweats and is now sprinting for the door? Or is it something else? What does it mean? More important, to whom is the disembodied voice speaking? I'm taking it in. It feels as though I'm supposed to respond, to assimilate this information and make use of it.

My baby started to cry. I sang a public health jingle I remember from TV when I was growing up: "Wash your hands after going to the bathroom/Wash your hands after changing baby too/ 'Cause we don't want to catch hepatitis/And we don't want hepatitis to catch you!/Or you!"

I don't know how to make fire, but this, this I've remembered for probably 25 years.

I caught a woman frowning in my direction. "Do you know," I said, "that there are a hundred million people in this country who have hepatitis C and don't even know it?"

"Really!" the woman said.

ONE THING I notice all the time—and plenty of others have also commented on this—is how angry people are. You can see it in their driving, in their posture. We are tense, strained, often lacking in good humor. All the time I hear people exhale loudly and swear under their breath. Most people, if you asked them, would say that life is too complicated. Yes, and too noisy and too distracting and too pointless and too rushed. Read Carl Honoré's *In Praise of Slowness*. We've lost the slow arts; we can't make fire. We struggle to form an independent thought. At the risk of sounding all Chicken Little, this is tragic—and will likely get worse.

In a world of plenty—snacks, amusements, music, cheaper car insurance, and free Spanish holidays—the one thing we're really lacking is silence. Along with silence goes freedom—the freedom to think your own thoughts, to do your own thing—to confront the world on your own terms and to grow. Maybe even the space to figure some things out, to find your place in the world.

"YOU'RE KIDDING, RIGHT?" a friend asked when I told him about the ASDA incident. "Smiling faces are those stickers on the ASDA products. You know? You're supposed to be all happy because the prices are so low."

I thought this was going to be one of those experiences that have no concrete explanation. I fancied some store employee gone mad with a microphone, rambling away until the manager hit him over the head with a discounted cricket bat. And this is what it comes to: a rational explanation. Except it's not so much rational as it is depressing.

"I'm supposed to be happy that some woman in Honduras has to sew a sleeve every 15 seconds? that her arms are so crippled she can't even lift her children? All so the shirt can cost four pounds?"

I wanted to hit him for spoiling my day, for making my Twilight Zone experience mundane and colorless. I want a list of Questions I Should Have Asked. I'm not sure I want the *actual answers*. If I had the answers, maybe all I'd have would be a big pile of nothing.

Is it any great surprise that unchurched people don't respond much to our overtures, our invitations for them to consider life's "big" questions? When you've done 30 Google searches over small questions in an hour, when you've been continually bombarded with issues that demand your immediate attention, when you can hardly remember your own name for all the piped music playing through the shops, all you want is to stop thinking.

I am often depressed that all the world seems to want from me is consumption. It wants me to buy. That is my function. That is all I am. "Won't someone challenge me?" I want to scream. "Give me a purpose? There are things I can do, you know." But the world just shrugs and reminds me that it takes Visa, MasterCard, and American Express.

Maybe it's also bad news for seekers when they get the impression that all God wants is church attendance, outward behavioral conformity, a dress code, and (mostly) verbal adherence to a somewhat abstract set of "beliefs."

Are we asking too much of people, as some suggest, or too little? There's no doubt organized religion has shot itself in the spleen in recent decades.

Whether or not the wound is fatal depends a great deal on how fast we treat it and with what kind of medicine.

I STILL DON'T know how to make fire. You'd think—seeing how I'm so obsessed with the topic—that I would have found out by now. I suppose I could. I keep saying I'm going on one of those survival weekends. But making fire isn't the issue. It's how each of us fears that we are all alone in the noisy world and that our existence is a house of cards. All it takes is a short unexpected puff to take it all down. What then? we ask ourselves desperately through the noise. What next?

You may long for another kind of life, but haven't a clue how to get it. Like me, you were in the bathroom when everyone voted this world with all its absurdities into existence. As a result, you may feel disenfranchised— what does any of this have to do with me?

Do this: Go into your garden, and if you don't have a garden, go to a park and sit under a tree. Find two sticks and rub them together until you realize that whoever suggested that as a way of making fire was having a laugh. Throw the sticks down in a fit of frustration. Take a deep breath, close your eyes, and allow your soul to ask that question—the one you're afraid to ask.

Christianity can sometimes feel like a marketing ploy. Someone's trying to sell you oceanfront property in Switzerland. They take Visa, MasterCard, and American Express. But I'm convinced that there is something real and eternal in our faith, something that we can find only individually, one at a time, as we make our way down separate paths—sometimes lonely or discouraged, but never alone.

It's time to get back to the basics, to finding our hearts, our roots, to connecting with our environment and finding a unique place in the world. That, pilgrim, is where you need to go.

"What are basics?" you ask. "How do I find my heart? What matters?"

Good questions. I can't answer them for you, so I'll share a little anecdote instead. I used to have a boss who smoked a great deal. Occasionally someone would ask to bum a cigarette. Then they'd want a light. My boss would get a devious glint in his eye, and he'd say, "You want me to smoke for ya too?"

Lots of people will happily give you a "cigarette"—even throw in a light and a crystal ashtray shaped like a turtle—but honey, you gotta "smoke" it yourself.

THROUGH THE KEYHOLE

ON A TRIP back to Seattle to visit my family, I found myself queuing in an alley with my brother for a cinema screening of *Das Kabinett des Doktor Caligari* with "live Theremin accompaniment." We noticed a man lying face-down in the alley, his body spread out wall-to-wall, like a lumpy rug. He was very still.

"Dude," my brother whispered. "Do you think that guy's dead?"

I frowned. "Dunno."

"Should we poke him?"

"What if he's sleeping? You know what they say about, uh, waking people who are asleep."

"I don't want to be in some newspaper report about how callous Seattleites are. 'A man lay dead in an alley for two weeks while thousands of moviegoers traipsed by chugging popcorn, and not one of them noticed he was dead until his corpse started to smell.' If he's dead, someone should call the coroner."

"OK then," I said. "Go for gold."

"You're older."

"But I'm a woman."

"Girls have fingers, no?"

I had a bright idea. "Get me a peppermint mocha."

"Focus, Beck, will you? We're still on the dead guy."

"No, I mean, head over to get the mocha and accidentally on purpose trip over the guy. If he's alive, he'll wake up, and he can't fault you for tripping. Remember, no whipped cream."

"OK. I'll get the mocha, but I'm tripping on the way back."

"No! You'll scald the poor guy!"

"I'll get you an iced mocha instead. Look, I just want to give him a few more minutes to wake up by himself. I don't want to humiliate myself for nothing."

Just after my brother left, the man began to stir. He sat up, looked around, and struggled to his feet. He brushed off the newspapers sticking to his stomach and lurched away, stumbling over rough spots on the pavement. I watched him with a strange ache in my stomach.

I'm so glad, I started to think, but I don't believe I ever finished the thought. The man rounded the corner at the end of the alley, and I couldn't see him anymore. Out of sight, out of . . . what was I saying?

My brother came back minutes later with drinks and napkins.

"So he was alive?" he asked.

"If he wasn't, you and I should probably be screaming and running. *Night of the Living Dead.*"

My brother gave me a look.

"Fine and dandy," I said. "Fit as a fiddle. Really drunk or strung out or crazy, though. Utterly tragic."

I took a sip of my mocha and shrieked. "Ew! Whipped cream? You let them add whipped cream? You want me to be fat or what?"

My brother took the lid off his own cup. "Aw," he cried in disgust. "Mine has whipped cream too. Morons. What is this, Mississippi? There's six bucks down the toilet."

"We're always getting ripped off."

"Yeah," my brother said. "Do we have the worst luck or what?"

MORE THAN ONCE, I've been mistaken for a homeless person—and also an Irish person (terrorist), but that's for another article. My friends would probably say it's because I'm not a snappy dresser. I often go out—where people can actually see me—wearing clothes that admittedly look like they might have spent the night in a dumpster. People in London have chucked spare change at me. In Paris a man once offered to take me to a homeless shelter, until I explained that I was freezing outside the Metro all night because I was too cheap to pay for a hotel. "Eediot!" the man exclaimed with a wave of his hand. Gotta love the French.

Every time I've been cold or hungry or slept rough, I've promised myself that when it's over, I'll be different. I'll change my attitude. Warmth, food, safety—I won't take these for granted. I'll savor them—actively think about how good they feel. But then somehow, every time, I forget. Good intentions slip away, and I start complaining about whipped cream. I turn into a person I'd totally want to pistol-whip. That's if I were the kind to own a "pistol," which I'm pretty sure is some kind of wood-working tool.

"EAT YOUR FOOD!" my mom used to bark when I refused lentils or green beans. "Think about all those starving kids in Ethiopia."

"Box it up," I'd say, turning up my nose and folding my arms with child-ish defiance. "Send it to them."

This is how we are—not only when we're 6 or 7, but all our lives. We're disdainful of our blessings—"Food? Hel-lo! I need a real blessing!"—and en-vious of others. No matter how many pictures you see of starving children with distended abdomens and vultures circling above, you'll still turn up your nose at green bean casserole or Spam or virtually any "food" served at the av-erage church potluck. "Yuck," people say. "I'm not putting that in my mouth."

IT MIGHT HAVE been on the same trip, or a different one—my ability to sequence is quite poor—that an old friend from school and I went to the an-nual "Street of Dreams" charity event. You pay 10 bucks—which goes to Seattle's Children's Hospital—to tour a selection of lavish homes, giving you the chance to poke through the kitchens, bathrooms, closets, home movie theaters, and wine cellars. Loyd Grossman, a U.K. television host who used to do a show called *Through the Keyhole,* during which contestants tried to guess who lived in a particular house by poking around for clues, would no doubt say in that pseudo-British accent of his, "Who would live in a house like this?" My response? "Duh, Loyd: a rich dude."

The houses featured outdoor fireplaces, showers the size of my bedroom, and walk-in closets supported by pillars—though I did note a startling lack of what I'd imagined to be the de rigueur home dungeon. Where are you supposed to keep your enemies? Sad when honorable traditions die.

Touring a huge fancy house has the same psychological effect as flipping through a glossy magazine—it makes your life shrink to a miserable pinpoint.

"I'm such a loser," I marveled, wandering through these perfect houses full of all the things I covet—art, big mirrors, indoor Jacuzzis, fluffy pillows, and marble countertops. If I lived in a house like that, there'd be no reason for me to be flawed. I'd have the space in which to be perfect. I could finally be the person I want to be—superorganized with a linen cupboard and a pantry and a calm, nonborderline psychotic demeanor. I could have one whole room full of beanbags where I'd jump around playing air guitar.

Guess who, funnily enough, I spent no time comparing myself to at all? Try the poor kids at Seattle's Children's Hospital—the ones with fetal alcohol syndrome, spina bifida, cystic fibrosis, childhood leukemia—kids who may die before they've ever caught a single snowflake on the tip of their tongue.

Imagine this: thousands, even millions, of people have lived and died without ever knowing what a full stomach feels like. They have never lived one day in safety. No one has ever loved them. These people have never owned enough shirts or trousers to necessitate a walk-in closet. Maybe the greatest wish they had when they were alive was not to step on a land mine or be sold into child prostitution. To feel lucky, these people wouldn't need a 20-foot TV and a screening room that seats 40 people on leather sofas with glass-top tables on which to place the Doritos and guacamole.

But it's not like this is news. We've seen the reports from the overseas correspondents on TV. We occasionally buy copies of *The Big Issue* from vendors in the high street out of guilt, but somehow we just ain't feeling it. We're always getting ripped off. Our jobs are unfulfilling, our houses too small, our bottoms too big, our cars too slow, our families dysfunctional, and our dreams dead. We keep getting pickles on our burgers after we clearly state, "No pickles." The world, you know what it does? It messes with us, that's what. It dangles these glittering prizes in front of our faces and then snatches them away with a sadistic laugh, leaving us hollow.

A MAN BEARS a large and heavy cross on his back. He drags it with him everywhere he goes. (It must make a day trip to Six Flags somewhat awkward.) One day the man trips and falls under the weight of the cross for perhaps the third time that week. "I can't take this anymore," the man huffs. He picks himself up, rubs some Neosporin on his grazed knee, and heads to the village church to speak to the priest.

"I can't carry this cross any longer," the man says. "It's impossible. It's so big, so heavy. It keeps tripping me up. I'm always falling. Help me, Father!"

The priest strokes his chin and considers the man. After a moment he gives a sharp nod of the head and says, "OK. You may exchange it for another."

"Thank you!" the man gasps, falling at the priest's feet in a heap of pathetic gratitude.

"Wait here for a moment," the priest says. He snaps his fingers, and two altar boys come running. Together they hoist the heavy cross onto their shoulders and drag it out of the room; the priest, following behind them, hums the theme song from *Friends*.

Sometime later the priest returns and asks the man to follow him down a long corridor. From his great ring of keys he selects an ornate golden one and opens a large wooden door. Behind the door is a room piled high with a tangle of enormous crosses.

The priest gestures with a sweep of his arm. "Choose," he says.

The man stands gaping, his gaze running desperately back and forth, up and down, over the pile. Finally he spots a small cross in the corner.

"That one," the man says.

The priest smiles. "My son," he says, "that is the cross you brought with you."

Perspective. The priest could have placed the man's cross in a room full of baby crosses, the kind you can wear comfortably on a delicate platinum chain around your neck. In that context, the man's cross would have appeared even more intolerable.

Obviously the priest was lying when he said the man could exchange his cross. No one can ever exchange their burden, but it's possible to realize that it could be much heavier, with sharper splinters. It's still possible to choose, sort of—as long as what you choose is what you already have. "You can have any color car you want," Henry Ford famously declared, "so long as it's black."

Faced with a choice like this, only a total idiot allows themselves to want racing green. But on Planet Earth, idiots are thicker than fog.

IT'S COMING UP to Christmas, the time of year when everyone spends too much, eats too much, and pretends to be jolly while inwardly facing the massive disappointments of their lives. Christmas puts all your failings, if you have them, in sharp relief. Your lack of money. The absence of friends and family—signified by your pathetic little pile of two Christmas cards—one of them from a car dealership.

Also, it's a simple way of marking time, a landmark event. Wow, it's Christmas again already? And yet I still don't have a partner or a job. I'm still not the totalitarian dictator of a small, rum-producing country. Even if your life is pretty good, it's not as good as it could be. If only life would quit messing with you. Anyone telling you you're lucky that you don't live in a box will likely be at the receiving end of a whole lot of scorn. Your scorn doesn't scare me, so allow me to be the one: You're lucky you don't live in a box.

Every year I plan certain perfections for Christmas, because, of course, I am a perfectionist—and a particularly sick and pathological one at that. Two years ago I decided that my son and I would make a gingerbread house. Even a kit with instructions didn't keep it all from going horribly wrong. The roof kept sliding off. Nothing would induce it to stay in place. I can't remember whether I actually threw the bowl of icing through my parents' sliding glass doors or whether I just wanted to—my grasp of the difference between real and imaginary has never been particularly strong—but suffice it to say that my behavior that afternoon was nothing you'd see on a good parenting video.

Problem is, I want my whole life to look like page 18 of *Martha Stewart Living* magazine.

"Dear God," I pray, "this year, please help me to be perfect." The room fills with low, chuckling laughter. "Baby steps," God says. "Remember? First you have to master *not throwing things.*"

WHEN I WAS a little kid, I was taught that we Americans were the luckiest people on earth. I don't care what anyone says about "trickle-down economics," the Reagan/Thatcher years were the best. During that period I was fortunate. Now, of course, I know the truth: the Norwegians are, in fact, the luckiest people on earth—winning the title by a narrow margin over the Swiss, whose attention to tidiness, while nice, is a tad too oppressive for anyone even a little bit normal.

Lots of people would, and do, say that Americans are deluded—not to mention arrogant—for having taught such conceits to their children. They laugh about how many small-town mid-Westerners still think America is the greatest country in the world. They call them provincial, naive, and simple-minded. Probably true, but I have another word, and it's perfectly printable. Try lucky.

If you think you're lucky, you are lucky. "Reality" is mostly in your own mind. That's why so many people think they're Elvis. Bless them, I say.

This Christmas, and for the next year—as a test—go ahead and delude yourself. Tilt your head and squint until you like what you see.

If you could be anyone in the whole history of the world, living or dead, pick yourself. Remember, you have everything you want. Every day you can find something that makes you smile. Don't trade crosses with anyone. Think about it. A black car is better than a skateboard. A skateboard is better than shoes. Shoes are better than ugly shoes. Ugly shoes are better than bare feet. Bare feet are better than no feet. No feet? There is always something to be thankful for.

Of course, you can't talk about this to everyone. Some people don't like positive people. If your friends knew, they'd throw rotten eggs at your skateboard and exclude you from social events. Keep the happy thoughts in a private corner of your mind and feed them often.

And remember, God promises that He won't give us more than we can handle. So when you think your cross is too big, keep in mind that God is in control. Trust me, He's way smarter than you are. If life hands you whipped cream, just shut up and swallow it. Someday you'll hopefully realize that it's not as bad as you think it is.

MARS AND VENUS

IF I WERE waiting in an airport after my flight was delayed, and I'd read all my books, drank coffee until my legs were trembling, walked through the metal detector four or five times with a pocketful of change, and purchased a really large Toblerone bar, I might start longing for human conversation. It is equally possible that I might fall asleep, dribbling on the vinyl chairs.

If I should wish to speak to someone, and I had the choice between a man and a woman, I'd pick the man. If I had the choice between a man, a woman, and a large crocodile, I'd choose the crocodile, but that's not so much an indicator of preference as it is good common sense. You never want to offend anyone with lots of sharp teeth and the ability to run surprisingly fast on rather short legs. Anyway, yeah, in the event that a large crocodile was not in the equation, I'd pick the man.

In spite of evidence suggesting that they start all the wars, commit most of the murders, view an absolutely terrifying amount of sickening pornographic material, have really smelly socks, and are rubbish at multitasking, I like men. I think they're interesting people, and it must be noted that in between the pillaging, they've discovered some good things (penicillin) and invented a few others (George Foreman grill).

I have a father, brother, husband, and two sons. I have only one mother and a few female friends—no sisters, no daughters—so overwhelmingly the people in my life are male, and I guess over time you become accustomed to their ways. You build up a tolerance, the way French people get used to certain kinds of unpasteurized cheese. A more cynical person might call it the Stockholm syndrome—identifying with your tormenters—but I honestly feel very little torment or oppression in my life. I am woman, hear me roar. Or whatever.

I've had no major problems communicating with men; so imagine my surprise when one of my wedding gifts, almost 11 years ago, was a book titled *Men Are From Mars, Women Are From Venus.*

"Huh," I said to myself, flipping through the book. "My parents always said I was from Hades. I wonder if that means I'm non-gender-specific." I began to hyperventilate, feeling the same dread I'd experienced some years earlier at the age of 13 when James Dobson told the story, on his radio broadcast, of a 14-year-old "girl" who suddenly, for no apparent reason, turned into a boy. Even now, as a so-called grown-up who has borne two children, I have never completely shaken the fear.

Repeating again and again, "Don't think about James Dobson and his sick story," never worked, so in order to distract myself from the horror of it all, I hunkered down on my beige sofa, amid the discarded wrapping paper, and read the book.

It's been 11 years, but pretty much all you need to know is right there in the title: men and women have so little in common that they might as well be from different planets. I hesitate to say "poppycock" straightaway—not even sure it's my kind of word—so first I'll point out that the author's premise is not completely without merit.

Men and women differ in three major areas—what I like to call the three S's. These are sports, shopping, and sex. There is much that could be said about these areas, but I'll spare you the *much*. Allow me to give just one example: guns. For the sake of my alliterative simplification, I file "guns" under "sport"—although in the right context, they might also fit under "shopping."

I think it's weird that little boys are obsessed with guns. Most men view this perspective as ridiculous.

"You have to let boys play with guns," my dad and brother both argue. "That's what little boys do."

"Right," I said. "So it's fine for little boys to 'murder'? Why don't we have little girls play—oh, I don't know—what do women go to jail for? I got it! Prostitution! Should little girls play hooker?"

My dad and brother shake their heads in sorrow at this argument. "That is so *not* the same thing," they say. "Where did I go wrong in raising you?" Dad adds.

Men and women are different, no doubt about that. Much has been made of men's spatial versus women's verbal abilities. I'm pretty sure I've seen a book somewhere called *Why Men Don't Iron*, but I haven't read it because I already know the answer. It's the same reason I don't iron: it's a hateful, awful chore. Save yourself now: buy wrinkle-free polyester.

The reason I'll happily rubbish the argument that men and women are from different planets is pretty simple: because they're not. We're all from this planet. We may have certain differences, as groups, in terms of aptitudes and interests, but we have a whole lot in common. Like the way we're subject to the laws of gravity. We have to eat. Men and women share most of the same organs and can suffer from mostly the same diseases. We know what it is to want things. We need meaningful tasks to fill our days. We love and hate. If you prick us, do we not bleed?

Some people are actually afraid to speak to members of the opposite sex because, get this—"They think so differently." No, they don't. Not that differently. Not so much so that—with a little effort—they can't be understood.

I'm sure this emphasis on the differences between sexes is a benevolent effort to make them both seem "special," but really, only individuals are special—never groups. Furthermore, by making people who are different from you fit into an "other" category, you dig a chasm that can become impossible to cross.

Ever play rock, paper, scissors? Imagine it's man, woman, human, and human is the thing that always trumps the other two.

Human is the thing we have in common; it makes us all, surprisingly, quite alike.

JUST A FEW weeks ago I went to a Saturday night concert put on by the London Youth Federation at the Advent Center. The music was so good, so inspiring, that I left with chills running up and down my spine—this, the feeling that I most crave, the unmistakable impression that I've just seen God.

"Did you hear that?" I raved to my husband all the way home. "They took some boring songs and made them wail! Now, that's worship. That was divine."

I was, I think, the only White person. Of course, I've been to "Black" churches before, and I've had Black friends visit my "White" church. And obviously, lots of Black and White people go to the same church, but apparently we still have some kind of big "cultural problem" here in Britain, particularly in terms of worship style. This is what I keep hearing. We don't like the same things.

Black churches don't start on time, and they go on too long. The music is loud and too "gospel" style. The preaching is repetitive, and the speakers often shout. The audience chatters. Everyone's always saying amen. Lots of women wear hats. What is up with that?

White churches are cold—and not in terms of the thermostat. The people can't sing and always appear bored—going through the motions. The preaching is dry—delivered in a monotone. The audience can't wait for the service to end so they can chug their decaf coffee and get out of Dodge.

Does that about sum up our "cultural differences"? You could probably add some of your own. I've heard plenty of people—Black and White—express the view that it is impossible for us to worship in unity. Better if we each go our own way—then everyone gets what they want and no one has to endure anything they don't like.

Put a sock in it, I say. If the man/woman thing teaches us anything at all, it's this: we have a God who enjoys fitting a square peg into a round hole. He doesn't make anything easy. If men and women were meant to be together for life, why can't they have similar attitudes toward some of the issues that can make lifelong monogamy difficult? Specifically, why do men have midlife crises that involve the purchase of Porsches? Yet we believe that God wants us to learn to love another person—different in some ways from ourselves—and that this is the work of a lifetime.

And don't forget—just as men and women are both from Planet Earth, so are Black and White people. We're not that different. Gravity, remember? With a little effort we can understand each other. But the key here is effort: we have to try.

THREE DAYS AFTER the London concert, I was in Durham for work. Having a few hours free, I chose to attend the evensong service at Durham Cathedral. This service was as much a contrast with the concert as anything could be. The church was so silent I could hear my own heart thumping. Men in purple robes led out as a formal choir sang in high, solemn voices. There were recitations. I stood up and sat down on cue, reading from a program as indicated. The service started and finished bang on the minute. If you were so inclined, you might call it overly formal or dry. But I left the cathedral that night and walked back to my hotel through the dark streets of Durham with the same chill running down my spine that I'd felt in London. There too, I saw God.

Nothing's better than watching a human being do what they do best. When we're good, we're really good. And when we're great, there's not a dry eye in the house.

"CAN WE ALL get along?" Rodney King asked, rhetorically, in 1991 after large-scale rioting in Los Angeles followed the acquittal of several police officers who had beaten him during the course of a traffic stop. This remark was greeted with great derision, and is still sometimes used sarcastically as an example, I guess, of a dumb question. Perhaps it's a simple question, but it actually strikes me as a pretty good one. The best questions are both deceptively simple and devilishly hard to answer.

Can we get along? I'm not asking if we can smile politely, but if we can worship together and accept and value each other's strengths. We'll need a willingness to see the positive and the admirable. We'll have to get over having things our own way. This is also what you do in marriage, or in any relationship you hope will last longer than three days.

Don't be afraid to consider new ideas, even those you've always thought of as "wrong." The worst thing about life is how it surprises you—that's also the best thing about life. You just never know when you might find yourself enjoying a delightful conversation with a large crocodile.

WARNING: THIS ARTICLE CONTAINS EXPLICIT MATERIAL

WHEN I LIVED in Hemel Hempstead, across from my house was a row of shops. Sometimes when people visited, they said things like "At least if you ever get tired of sitting in your small house you can look out the window and observe the frenzied activity at the shops."

I can't think of anything more dull than watching people go in and out of shops—even the way paint dries can have a certain charming unpredictability—so I never engaged in this particular activity. On the three occasions in which uniformed police officers knocked on my door wanting information on "serious incidents" from across the road, I was unable to be of service.

"Do I look like the sort of loser who has nothing better to do than look out the window?" I snarled, standing in the doorway in a tattered flannel robe and Barney slippers. The police officers hung their heads in shame.

One of the shops was a post office/newsagent run by a severe-looking elderly man in a turban who called me "luv," and his wife, who was unfortunately robbed at gunpoint a few years back. They sold the usual corner shop variety of crisps, paper clips, newspapers, greeting cards, notebooks, and, well, porn.

"Are you sure this is a real post office?" my father always asked. Where we're from, the only things present in a post office are packing tape, boxes, stamps, and gun-crazed, stressed-out postal workers. A post office is a federal building—and last time I checked, the postmaster general was not one William J. Clinton. So, no porn.

For years I noticed that the entire top shelf of the magazine section was dedicated to what are sometimes delicately referred to as "men's entertainment" magazines. Does anyone else think it's funny (funny/strange AND funny/ha-ha) that "women's entertainment" magazines contain recipes and knitting patterns? Of course, for a woman the sight of a strange man naked isn't so much entertainment as cause for alarm.

One day, because this is the kind of person I am—inquisitive—and also because I was stuck in a 15-minute pre-Christmas posting queue—I decided to count the magazines. There were a total of 22. Twenty-two. Given that this is a post office and not a specialist purveyor of pornographic materials, this seems like a lot. As a quick comparative analysis, the shop stocks only six kinds of potato chips.

So is it worse to look at porn or eat too many high-fat/high-salt snacks? One will kill you faster, that's for sure, so maybe it depends on your definition of "worse."

I was just finishing counting when Mr. Vishawparkaash offered to help the next person in line, which was me.

"Twenty, twenty-one, twenty-two," I said triumphantly, tearing my eyes from a rather tacky and poorly printed cover and turning my attention over to the proprietor. "Right. That's in order. I'll just mark it on my clipboard here." It was then that I realized I wasn't carrying a clipboard. I have never, even once, carried a clipboard, and right then and there, I put that on my list of things to do before I die.

"I'll need to post these to the Planet Krypton," I said, trying to distract him from my weirdness with the porn.

Mr. Vishawparkaash scowled.

THERE ARE SOME Christians who believe that you should speak up and protest whenever you see anything wrong in the world.

Oddly, though, these Christians typically notice only a very narrow slice of all the things that are actually wrong. They pick out sexual immorality, abortion, blasphemy, and witchcraft, as seen in popular children's books such as the Harry Potter series. Last year there was a big Christian stink about *Jerry Springer: The Opera,* because of "blasphemy." I found that odd. When was the last time you heard Christians mounting a protest against the *Jerry Springer Show* (TV) because it mocks and exploits poor, ignorant, dentally challenged, overweight people who live in trailers and subsist on Twinkies? *Fat and stinky, toothless too/Fit right in down at the zoo/ Jesus loves the ugly people in the park.* (You sing those lyrics to the tune of "Jesus Loves the Little Children," by the way.)

Just like it's hard to decide which charity to support when there are so many and you can't help all of them and a few don't seem particularly worthwhile (like Dog Trust), it's also difficult to decide what's worth making a flap over. To flap or not to flap—this is the question.

What should I do about the—count 'em—22 porn magazines in my local post office? Should I stand outside with a big fancy sign hanging over my shoulders? collect signatures? write a letter to my local MP? Maybe I could hire a megaphone and shout rhyming slogans at passers-by: *I'm a Christian, reborn/I don't want no stinking porn!*

Some people think the world would be a better place if we stopped thinking and started taking action. But I'm not so sure about that. Right now I'm leaning toward think more, act less. Most of the time, the only action required—the only one that can possibly do any good or effect any real change—is the firing of the neurons in that thick, lumpy thing between your ears. *One, two, three, four/We all need to think more. Five, six, seven, eight/There's no need to legislate.*

At age 21, when I was still young enough to consider myself open-minded, I visited a place called the Sex Museum. As you may have already guessed, it is located in the historic city of Amsterdam. Back then I thought I was pretty cool and tough, and I didn't think anything could possibly shock me. Totally hard-core. Also, I suppose I expected the museum to be sort of artistic—full of, you know, art. It wasn't. It was full of porn. The difference between the two can be subtle, but after much thought, I'll offer the following distinction: Rarely is it necessary for an individual, when viewing art, to wear sunglasses and a hat pulled down low over the eyes so as not to be recognized.

After spending far too long in the museum—and in this museum, five minutes would have been too long—I stepped outside feeling utterly sick and repulsed. I thought about becoming a hermit, and I have long considered seeking treatment for posttraumatic stress disorder as a result of that one afternoon.

"What do you know about that?" I mused to myself—still slightly dazed—while waiting for a train at the Amsterdam station later that night. "I'm a puritan."

IN THE MID-EIGHTIES, when I was in my teens, the Parents Music Resource Centre (PMRC), headed by Tipper Gore, waged a campaign of censorship against explicit content in record albums (known by the early humanoids as "cassette tapes"). One of the main features of this movement was putting labels on albums so parents would know whether they were explicit and in precisely what way (violent, sexual, occult, etc.).

The result of all this controversy and talk about the evilness of rock music is not hard to conjure. Kids became more desperate than ever to listen to the albums with the stickers. I am a living testimony: without the stickers, I doubt very much whether I'd be the sort of person who could—if my life depended on it—recite from memory most of the album *As Nasty as They Wanna Be,* by 2 Live Crew.

The great Steven Tyler, vocalist for the legendary seventies rock-and-roll band Aerosmith, made an acceptance speech at an awards ceremony in which he sarcastically thanked Tipper Gore and the PMRC for ensuring that all he had to do was throw in a few four-letter words and his albums would sell an extra million copies.

This is funny and sad. Funny because it's true, and sad because the people behind PMRC were no doubt earnest, decent individuals who hoped to make the world a better place, but they unwittingly steered a whole lot of people right toward the very cliff they'd wanted to keep them from falling off.

During this same time period, at my school and at church events, speakers would often lecture about drugs and sex and involvement with the occult.

They tried to scare us into making better choices than they had, but to me the stories sounded exotic and glamorous, much more interesting than my suburban schoolgirl life. "I used to run drugs across the Mexican border for a Colombian cartel," one man said. "Then I got caught and went to federal prison."

Wow, I thought, *sounds great!*

MAYBE IT WOULD have been better for me if I'd never been to the Sex Museum or listened to 2 Live Crew. Then again, maybe not. You can't necessarily ensure that your experiences will be entirely sanitary. What you can hope is that what happens to you on your journey takes you toward God. Perhaps if you never saw an ugly, perverse world you'd feel no need for anything better. You'd do all the "right" things while drifting further from the One who can give you life. People do grow up, and if they're fortunate, somewhere along the way the difference between right and wrong—between darkness and light—hits them in the stomach and knocks the wind out of them. They fall, blinded.

You don't know a thing until you know it. Sometimes a hard-core tough girl goes into a yucky museum and comes out a puritan. It isn't only the beautiful things that transform you—it's also the ugly and how you respond to them.

Does this mean that Christians shouldn't speak out against things that are wrong in the world? Well, I don't know. Let me put it this way: virtually everything is wrong with the world. So ask yourself this: just how much time do you have? Do you really want to use the small window of opportunity you might have to be heard spouting off about Jerry Springer or some dirty pictures in the post office or a children's book series? When we do this, we give the impression, once again, that we Christians are the kind of people who are comfortable being only against things.

"But do you know how many people in this world are addicted to Internet porn?" you ask. No, and I don't want to. I try very hard not to be scared in elevators as I stand next to people who, to me, look very much like Internet porn addicts. Anyway, my freaking out and wearing a cardboard sign and forming arguments won't necessarily do anything to change other people's behavior. It might even create more Internet porn addicts.

"What about the story of the boy throwing the jellyfish back into the ocean?" you say. " 'You'll never make a difference,' people told him. 'Made a difference to that one,' the boy wisely said. What do you say to that?"

I say this: that story works only if you're talking about jellyfish. Too bad human beings aren't so simple. If only there was one swift, repetitive action that would work on all of them, rendering their problems obsolete. You can't just throw people into the ocean, much as you might like to. You have to ask them first. They have to sign a series of legal waivers. Even then, my legal team assures me, you're probably still looking at some serious jail time.

The following story seems to be something of an urban legend. There is some dispute as to whether it actually happened, but it's the kind of thing that easily could happen, so hey, that's good enough for me. After the Exxon Valdez oil spill in Alaska, and a very expensive cleanup operation, a group of environmentalists and other nature lovers got together on the shore to release a sea otter back into the wild. The people cheered as the otter was released, then were horrified when seconds later, in front of their very eyes, it was gobbled up by a killer whale.

"Making a difference" isn't always a positive thing. It just means that after you and your funky new ideas come along, things are different. Richard Reid, the shoe bomber, made a difference. You can observe it every time you take off your shoes in airport security and smell your own stinky socks.

Maybe it's better simply to be the difference—as a popular slogan/cheesy cliché puts it—and see if that makes the world glow a little brighter. (Warning: a desire to make the world glow brighter is, under no circumstances, an excuse for the use of unauthorized radioactive materials.)

DOWN WITH THE CLOWN

IT WAS A lazy, mindless evening, and I was doing some "research" on my computer. As it sometimes happens, one Google query led to another, and I inexplicably came across a Detroit-based rap group called Insane Clown Posse (ICP). ICP is made up of two men, both named Joseph. Professionally they are known as "Violent J" and "Shaggy 2 Dope," respectively. As their group name suggests, they dress like evil clowns. Yeah, it surprised and disturbed me, too.

"Oi!" I shouted to my husband across the house—my voice only partially audible because my mouth was full of cheesy puffs—"Ever heard of a rap group called 'Insane Clown Posse'?"

"What?"

I pushed the "food" into my left cheek because it was too soon to swallow. If you want to be in possession of a healthy constitution, you must chew your cheesy puffs no less than 100 times before swallowing.

"Never mind. Just answer me this: Do you think it's possible that there is some kind of—oh, I don't know—top-secret organization that kidnaps you while you're sleeping, steals your nightmares through the use of high-tech equipment, and then offers those nightmares lucrative recording contracts?"

SO YEAH, LIKE a lot of people, I don't care too much for clowns. Nor mimes. Nor those big walking stuffed animals at amusement parks.

I'm a little afraid to be this vulnerable since recently a reader, misunderstanding my highly sophisticated sense of humor, wrote me a letter complaining that I "lack proper respect for the police." This could not be further from the truth: when I'm not busy respecting the police (and folks, it's a full-time job), I'm trawling Luton in a neon jacket actually impersonating an officer of the law. That's how much I like and (let's not forget) respect the old Bill. Especially Inspectors Morse, Frost, Lynley, Tennison, and that really cool—and kinda cute—guy who goes to this church I sometimes visit.

So let's make sure we're clear. With regard to the aforementioned clowns, it isn't so much that I don't respect them as it is that I just loathe them. Or hate them, if you prefer.

Yeah, boss, I know it's a strong word. And here's a long word: "coulrophobia." You guessed it: that's Farsi for "fear of clowns." I'm hyperventilating as I write this, but it must be done. As Master Yoda said, "Fear is the path to the dark side. Fear leads to anger; anger leads to hate; hate leads to suffering."

Clowns, in case you were wondering, lead to balloons. Balloons lead to cotton candy. Cotton candy leads to a big blue sticky mess. You don't know suffering until you've got that caked in your hair.

"THE FANS CALL themselves 'Juggalos,'" I ranted to a friend. "*Juggalos!* Why? Why would they do that? Isn't it fearful enough, the prospect that others might label you with a silly-sounding name? The girls are called 'Juggalettes.' You should see the stuff for sale on eBay. T-shirts for 100 bucks! People are obsessed with this stuff!"

"Which people?" my friend asked. "Besides you."

"According to my Internet research, ICP fans are people from 'all walks of life.' But nobody from my walk of life. People I know may not be perfect, but at least they don't waste their lives following some quasi-religious clown rap group."

"Uh-huh," my friend said.

"They say they're 'down with the clown.' They believe in a force called the 'Dark Carnival,' which I think is supposed to be God. If you're a good Juggalo, when you die you go to Shangri-la! How lame is that? Also, I'm sorry, but two guys do not a 'posse' make. I can forgive a multitude of errors, but there's simply no excuse for slap-dash vocabulary."

"The world is a weird and wonderful place," my friend said, making me suspect she'd been reading *A Letter Concerning Toleration* behind my back.

"Oh, get over it," I said. "Clowns are not wonderful. Clowns are just weird. And scary. And not funny. Why would a person willingly submit to a label that involves clowns? For that matter, why would a human—free, dignified, and sovereign beings that we are—submit to a label of any kind? Why would you want to walk around calling yourself anything at all?"

"You mean like 'Christian'?"

I AM ALLOWED to make disparaging remarks about clowns because I used to be one. That's how it works: anything you either currently are or at some point in your past used to be, you can make fun of, and no one can get huffy. For future reference, the groups I can make rude comments about are as follows: women, Americans, mothers, CIA operatives, fast-food workers, teachers, and clowns. The people I respect in both word and action? The police.

When I was 14—right on the cusp of becoming the most fearsome creature the world has yet to see, the 15-year-old girl—I was a part of something called clown ministry. This involved the entire eighth-grade class wearing clown costumes and acting stupid in front of poor trapped individuals in nursing homes, institutions, and day-care centers. The acting stupid part came to us somewhat naturally. For everything else, our leader provided makeup, balloons, buckets of water, and a van to haul us around in.

FYI: I was a hobo clown. And no, the whole clown thing didn't freak me out in this case because I was a clown, just like I wouldn't be frightened of myself if I were a gigantic spider. Duh.

Once we were "ministering" at a home for people with special needs, and there was a poor man sitting in the corner wearing an American football helmet and whacking his head against the wall. This made me feel terrible, and I thought I'd cheer him up by leering in amusing clown fashion and clumsily pretending to juggle.

Not 30 seconds into my act he started to laugh. Encouraged, I pranced around acting *even weirder.* He laughed louder. And louder. And pretty soon it became apparent, from the terrified look in his eyes that this was frightened laughter. It quickly morphed into a screaming giggle, the kind that makes you feel as though you might not survive the next 10 seconds. It was contagious. Pretty soon all the people were screaming. I had this sinking feeling that we weren't so much being part of the solution, but I didn't know what to do. Nobody else did either, so we just kept prancing around, juggling and hitting each other with gigantic soft mallets until the director told us to leave. "Thank you," she shouted over the din. "That was lovely."

In defense of the entire eighth-grade class, let me point out that we quite faithfully followed the first rule of many "ministries," clown or otherwise: Never let the fact that you're freaking people out get in the way of "spreading the good news."

"Clown ministry," our leader told us repeatedly, in the requisite perky voice, "is about communicating the gospel in a way that is fresh, fun, and—most important—nonthreatening."

Say it as many times as you want, Chuck. Doesn't make it so.

As Shakespeare once wrote, "A tortoise by any other name still gets squashed on an afternoon jaunt across the highway."

ORIGINALLY THEY WERE the Inner City Posse, later regrouping under the clown motif, collecting followers, and becoming what some think of as a dangerous religious cult for disenfranchised teenagers. Their music is supposed to be "a metaphor for the choice each of us has with regard to how we spend our afterlife."

ICP fans uniformly claim that the group brings great meaning to their lives and dismiss critics by saying they don't "properly understand" the meaning of the music. They tend to make this point in a fairly hateful manner, not appearing to deal well with constructive criticism. This is why it's just as well they don't know I live in a stone fortress here in the Outer Hebrides. *Brrr.* It's cold.

And after a brief survey of the music (including titles such as "I Stab People," "Still Stabbin'," and "Southwest Strangla"), I'd be disinclined to accept that ICP has anything to do with belief in God, or that there's any way—untutored—you would ever suspect it did.

Doesn't it make you wonder about the whole concept of "belief"? You can "believe" anything you want. Your beliefs can seem rational and appealing (probably not if you're a Juggalo—sorry). Your beliefs can make you look like a good person. Your beliefs might even be true.

But so what? How does it matter if you "believe" good things but do bad ones? If you say you're "ministering" but really you're just making people scream? If you call yourself a Christian or a "nice person" just so you can coast beneath the radar, so no one will challenge you? And if they do, you can say: "I'll have you know, I'm a very caring person." Regardless of evidence to the contrary, people will be expected to accept this. If they don't, they're judgmental.

It seems that no matter what we call ourselves, no matter how hard we try to dress our actions and motives up in pretty ribbons, no matter who we are or what we claim to "believe," we manage to fall short. Why is that? Is there something wrong with our beliefs or something wrong with us?

Maybe we humans are just pathetic wrecks who need to create meaning in our lives because otherwise there is none. Maybe we lie because we can't bear the truth.

"I never would have taken you for a nihilist," one of my friends said.

"Oh, I don't know if I'd go so far as to call myself a 'Nile-ist,' " I said modestly. "I mean, sure, I like Egypt, but I'm not what you'd call an expert or anything."

WHEN A SELF-PROFESSED Juggalo does something bad—like Jacob B. Robida did when he killed several people and then himself—the others are quick to point out that the person "has no idea what being a Juggalo is really about."

That's the same thing we say about self-confessed Christians when they (circle the applicable verb/phrase): lie, cheat, murder, gossip, have affairs, beat their kids, or "act stuck-up." We make excuses, not only for ourselves but for others. And what choice do we have? People are all around either ignoring us or asking, "What do you have to show for yourself?" And too often we give them a leaflet with a list of our "beliefs." I can imagine a person frowning at such a leaflet with confusion. *I don't want to know what you believe*, he thinks. *I want to know what you are.*

Beliefs are good, so long as they provide a map for your life rather than a shelter to hide under. Often they end up as little more than a cover for a life that lacks substance. Instead of actually having to do or be, you can just "believe." You can tell yourself some awfully big lies. You can waste your whole life spouting empty words and smiling until, at some point, your cover is blown.

As Confucius wrote: "A dishonest squirrel hides his acorns beneath the tall willow."

NO MATTER WHAT Juggalos might say about the great joy and light that ICP music brings to their lives, it isn't at all hard to see why their fruit is sometimes rotten. Violence and negativity results in (surprise!) violence and negativity. The end product of their beliefs is ugly because the substance itself appears to be primarily about stabbing people.

Not so with Christianity. We have a good road map—the best. We just aren't always great at following it—at "being" rather than merely professing. Our lives, at some point, have to be about more than just a label.

It's a cliché, but living an authentic life really is about whom you know. Instead of asking "What would Jesus do?" try talking direct: "Jesus! What do You think I should do?" Stop making excuses. Learn to listen.

MY HUSBAND HAS a number of irritating habits, such as leaving piles of orange peels on the floor and reading over my shoulder when I'm trying to type. You can see why my writing has a nervous, disjointed quality. But sometimes he rubs my shoulders, so I'm not inclined to complain too much.

"So who's the 'cute' policeman?" he asked.

"Duh," I said. "Inspector Morse. But you don't have to worry about him. He's a character from the television. Also, he's like 900 years old."

"No, I mean the one you said goes to some church you visit."

"Oh," I said. "That. I was probably making that up. I do from time to time, you know. Gives the story flow. Or it might really be true. I get confused. So much to remember."

"Uh-huh."

"Anyway, you've still got nothing to worry about. I believe in fidelity."

"Is that the real believe or is it 'believe' in quotation marks?"

"The action word. If I meant 'believe' in quotes, I'd do the universal 'quote' sign. Index and middle fingers of both hands, held to the face, bent at the knuckle two times only, as the word is spoken. But a person will never do that. It looks cheesy, for one thing. Also, most of us lack the kind of self-awareness that allows us to see our true motivations.

"At any rate, the insights I've offered in this article are to be used in your private spiritual life—not as a way of working out who's a liar. As for whether or not I really believe in fidelity or whether I only 'believe,' well, watch this space. If I'm still sitting here in 50 years, I guess you'll know."

"If you're going to sit there for 50 years, I guess maybe I should get you a cushion then."

"Ah," I said. "That would be nice."

A JOURNEY OF
A THOUSAND MILES

"A journey of a thousand miles begins with a single step."
—Chinese proverb

ONE AUTUMN DAY when I was 18 years old, my parents and I loaded up two cars with clothes, pictures, duvets, and pillows at our home in the suburbs of Seattle.

We drove convoy-style over the mountains and across the desert to a small oasis called Walla Walla ("the town so nice they named it twice"). Walla² is home to three colleges, one state penitentiary, a wonderful European-style café called Merchants, and an astonishing number of gun racks on the backs of pickup trucks.

I didn't want to leave my home with the lake and mountain views. I'd worked all summer for a family in our neighborhood, taking care of their baby, and it was fun and familiar. My wacky writing persona may suggest otherwise, but I am a creature of habit. I like the familiar grooves, the trodden paths.

There was just one thing I feared more than going away to college, and that was being a "loser." If I stayed home and didn't study and babysat a kid and sponged off my parents, I'd be a loser, so I got into the car and drove over the mountains and through the desert, taking directions from my father who was in the passenger seat making sure I learned the route and drove at a safe and economical 63 miles per hour.

"Never miss a class," my dad offered during the course of a friendly-but-pointed lecture. I include this because it's fine advice. Put another way, it goes like this: show up.

While driving, I consoled myself with plans of how I'd spend the next few days—before freshman orientation began and my roommate arrived. I planned to fold and iron my clothes and organize them by color, to hang my pictures, to make the bland dorm room into a home I could love and where I'd feel safe.

Occasionally, for reasons that remain a mystery to me, I enter phases of life during which I pursue organization with the single-minded determination of a seagull at St. Ives bent on stealing your warm, delicious potato pasty. Redemption, I'll tell myself, comes in the form of alphabetizing, color-coding, folding, and filing. This is both true and not true. Sometimes redemption comes in the form of sitting in a great mess and not caring; of laughing even though you can't find a matching pair of socks or your debit card. It's all about the timing. As Kenny Rogers might say, "You gotta know when to hold 'em, know when to fold 'em, and know when to throw 'em in a smelly heap on the floor."

SOME SIX HOURS later—including a stop for breakfast at a roadside diner—we arrived to find that an ubiquitous "disgruntled employee" had destroyed the housing application records of several dozen students. I'm sure I'm not alone in expressing relief that said worker didn't employ the customary "disgruntled" approach of discharging a firearm of some sort in a hamburger restaurant—even though that wouldn't have had half the negative effect on me personally.

The college was faced with an interesting mathematical problem—the same sort dealt with daily by large airlines—more seats than seats, you might say. But when airlines overbook and are forced to bump someone, the lucky passenger gets either a free ticket or a significant sum of cash.

Not so at this "college of higher education," as Sir Alan Sugar from the British version of *The Apprentice* might disdainfully dub it. They assigned me to a depressing low-slung Norman Bates-style motel with a mildewed shower curtain and a double bed that I was expected to share with my roommate.

"What?" my mother kept asking incredulously. "She has to *share* a bed? Why, if we put her up in Washington State Penitentiary—which I'm pretty sure we could do at the taxpayers' expense—she'd at least get her own bed!"

"And a big yard to exercise in," my father added. "Three meals a day."

"I hear they have an excellent law library," the housing coordinator answered wearily.

My parents stalled as long as they could. We had a late lunch at Sea Galley. They helped me unpack—loading all my things into a corner of the motel room.

"I don't like it here," I said, my lower lip trembling like a 4-year-old's on her first day of nursery school. "I don't want to stay."

My parents, while sympathetic, are also the same people who had already left me two years earlier at boarding school under a raining barrage of threats and curses. "I hate you! I'm never speaking to you again! Consider this the first day of my hunger strike!"

I stood at the door and bawled as they drove away. I didn't find out until later that of course they too cried most of the way home, just as almost everyone does on passing an important milestone.

As much as a part of my life was beginning on that day, a part of theirs was ending. And vice versa too, actually.

What is it about milestones that is so hard? The thought that nothing will ever be the same? Fear of failure? Fear of the milestone getting inadvertently caught around your neck and dragging you to rest at the bottom of a clear stream? How would a milestone, firmly planted into claylike soil, get caught around a person's neck? Is this the work of organized crime syndicates? Do milestones in fact get caught around people's necks, or is that some other kind of stone?

"It's an albatross, actually," a good friend offered. "To have an albatross around your neck refers to an oppressive influence from which it is difficult to escape."

"What kind of stone is an albatross?" I asked.

FOR TWO DAYS I didn't leave the motel room. I didn't even open the curtains. I sat on my bed and watched the TV and read books and slept. The woman from the desk—small-town-nosy-but-nice—knocked on the door and tried to coax me outside. She gave me a bowl of green apples, and for two days I ate nothing else. I didn't want to go to the cafeteria and face the eyes of strangers. I was too demoralized to get in my car and drive around. I was even a little afraid I might get lost and have to (gasp!) ask for directions.

The longer I stayed in the room, the harder it became to open the door and step outside. The outside became this looming thing of my imagination, full of unspeakable horrors. I jumped at every noise—people walking past my window, the idling of cars. Because I kept the curtains drawn I couldn't see what was happening outside, and I relied on my imagination to fill in the blanks. Once, someone—probably by mistake—turned the handle of my door. "Go away!" I shouted, and then I lay flat on my back, my heart palpitating, for hours, listening for the slightest hint that the "intruder" might be back with a hacksaw or a credit card.

On the third day I started getting cabin fever. I took a shower and dressed myself in a Ralph Lauren polo shirt and shorts outfit that I was especially proud of. I fixed my hair with a wide red Alice band.

It wasn't much of an excursion.

I scampered to my car and drove just a few blocks out of town to the Red Apple Market. I bought myself a bag of Tim's Cascade Style Potato Chips in (hot!) Jalapeño flavor to supplement my all-apple diet, and then rushed back to the motel, where I once again barricaded myself behind the faux wood door and enjoyed the benefit of air-conditioning against the sweltering heat of a Walla Walla summer.

The next day it was easier to open the door. I got dressed and went to church. About the time a young man my age fell in step with me and introduced himself, I realized that I would be OK. And I was. For the next four years I was regularly forced to do things I didn't want to do. Set my alarm for 4:00 a.m. to study for exams. Give speeches. Write poetry and read it aloud. Learn German naval history. Learn German.

I got my degree, and that, boys and girls, is how I came to be the highly successful individual you can see in your mind's eye: mildly cross-eyed and hunchbacked, wearing an old bathrobe, sitting at the computer with a mouthful of cheesy puffs. Hey, if I can do it, so can you!

JUST YESTERDAY, WHILE I was lacing up my running shoes for my morning jog, it occurred to me how easy it is to have great dreams and goals but how difficult it is to do the day-to-day unheralded and unglamorous work necessary to carry you over 1,000 miles of rocky and sometimes inhospitable terrain. It's hard to stand up, face the distant horizon, and declare, "Today I will go as far as my wobbly legs will take me; tomorrow I will rise, step, and repeat. And for all I know, my effort will come to nothing. This could all be in vain."

I am currently in training to climb Mount Rainier, in Washington State, this summer. If I make it, I'll be pretty chuffed, and be warned—you'll never hear the end of my boasting. But in order to climb Mount Rainier, I have to jump through a number of unappealing hoops. I have to tie knots in the dark with my eyes closed. I have to run every day to build my endurance.

My daily route is only about two miles. Some of the route is uphill, some downhill, and some flat, but you'll never guess what the hardest and most hateful part of that jog is. Try, opening my front door.

I'm always too tired. I never feel like jogging. I try to find ways to avoid going. And at the moment, it's pretty easy. I don't huff and puff or stop or pretend to tie my shoes in order to get a breather. Still, jogging is less pleasant than, say, sitting in my chair sipping a cup of tea.

Whether you're talking about a journey of 1,000 miles or a quick jaunt around the block, that first step is somehow never easy. It's simpler and less fearful to stay where you are, with the door bolted shut.

You can dream of success as an AIDS-curing research doctor or a Grammy-winner singer or a gold medalist in curling at the Winter Olympics. Maybe, like me, all you ever wanted was to make sure you weren't a total loser. But whatever it is you're looking for, you'll find it faster if you open the door. You'll go farther if you start moving now while there's plenty of daylight.

The first step will never be any easier than it is right now. So go on—it might be painful and hard, but if you do it quick, like ripping off a bandage, you'll realize it wasn't so bad. I promise you: it hurts for only a second.

A BETTER MAN

I HAVE A special box. It is colorfully painted and wood-burned. Around the edges the phrases "Dream Big," "Follow Your Heart," and "Believe in Yourself" are etched in curly script. This box was a gift from my parents for my thirtieth birthday. In addition to being a work of art, the purpose of the box is to provide a place for me to keep sentimental tokens.

Inside the base is etched "My Stuff," and for a while, when I first got it and my parents were visiting, it was full of everything *but* my stuff. Passports. Airline tickets. Even now I tend to put things in the box that I desperately need to keep track of rather than things that hold a special meaning for me.

Even so, I have locks of my children's hair in my box. Inexplicably, I recently noticed a specimen bottle containing my husband's gallstones—removed by surgery almost four years ago. *Gross*, I thought, but I left them there. If I were to die and strangers went through my things, would they find it strange that I kept my husband's gallstones in a special box? Or would it make me seem a bit like Angelina Jolie?

One important thing in the box is something I've held precious for just about half my life. It is a watch with a wristband made of genuine U.S. pennies. It stopped working maybe 15 years ago, and the face is cracked. I've tried replacing the batteries a few times, and for a week or two the watch runs, but then, for some reason, it dies again. I'm not normally the kind of person to hang on to a nonfunctioning item, but I will keep this watch for as long as my forever lasts.

How I came to own this watch is partly a mystery—mostly because of my faulty memory. I can confirm the following facts: (a) I saw this watch on a shopping trip at the Everett Mall—30 miles north of Seattle—and I coveted it; (b) I returned about a week later and used my father's Visa card to purchase the watch for $45 (plus sales tax); and (c) it has been mine ever since.

The mystery, the part I can't seem to remember, is the short, straight line between a and b. Would I have actually asked my father to buy me the watch? Not likely. I can imagine Dad's face at the mention of a penny watch: "What do you need *that* for?" It wasn't like I didn't have a watch.

So I don't remember the conversation we must have had. All I can re-call is my shock and delight when my dad pulled out his wallet and handed me the credit card.

"Just the watch, right?" he said.

"Right! Wow, thanks!"

It was better than cash, because it was an expression of trust. Faith, even. Faith that I, a decidedly untrustworthy teenager with too much makeup, funny hair, a nasty attitude, and the obligatory dodgy boyfriend in tow, would do the right thing—would act responsibly. It was an expression of faith that I would not embark on a rampant spending spree with my friends or flee across the border to Canada or purchase an RV or airplane tickets to Hawaii.

I'm proud to say that out of the many tests that have come my way over the past 30-odd years—many of which I've failed rather miserably—I passed this one with a perfect score. I remember signing my name on the dotted line and putting the word "daughter" in brackets just as the salesclerk told me to—back in the day before the advent of chip and pin, fingerprinting, and retina scans.

She handed me a small, white box with my watch inside, nestled on a bed of cotton and tissue. I slipped the credit card into my pocket and went straight to the car. I traveled straight home and proudly marched upstairs to give the card and a copy of the receipt to my dad.

When I look at my watch now, I think about two things. Number one: how amazing it feels to be the object of another's trust. Number two: how number one is true only when—by your actions—you earn that trust. How bad would I feel if, after my father trusted me with his Visa card, I'd repaid that trust by throwing a keg party on a yacht, putting it all on plastic?

Wow. Most of the time I make myself sick. I'm surprised I can manage to drag my sorry self around. Watch this space.

IN THE FILM *As Good as It Gets* Jack Nicholson plays cranky, rude, obses-sive-compulsive Melvin who falls for exhausted server Carol. She lives a des-perate life with a sick young son, and thinks that Melvin is a freak—a fact she makes clear in no uncertain terms. Away from home to support a friend in crisis, they end up having dinner in a restaurant, allowing Melvin to promptly display his usual unbearable characteristics.

"Give me a compliment," Carol says, furious and exasperated. "Say something nice, or I'm outta here."

"When you said we could never be together," Melvin replies, "the very next morning I started taking my pills [referring to the medication he's been prescribed for his mental illness]. That's my compliment to you."

"I don't get how that's a compliment for me," she says.

He leans back, grins, and delivers this knockout line: "You make me want to be a better man."

PEOPLE ARE ALWAYS working on improving themselves. That's what people do. "Build a better mousetrap," Ralph Waldo Emerson is credited with saying, "and the world will beat a path to your door." We imagine people will also beat a path to our door if we build a better "me." We're always being hectored about all the ways in which we can improve: Thinner Thighs in Thirty Minutes, etc. But here's a question: are thinner thighs *better?* Let me put it another way: at what point do you know you've actually improved— that you are, in fact, a better mousetrap? Better like how?

Example: for as long as I can remember, complete strangers have occasionally approached, shoving their faces into my field of vision and commanding, "Smile!"

I don't have an accurate picture of how I look walking around, but if this offers any kind of hint, I guess I must cut a rather morose figure. I could conclude that if I want to be a better me, I should start looking happier. Change my personality. Become chipper, chirpy. But here's the rub: suppose I went to all that effort—would I actually be better, or would I just be different?

I STARTED SMOKING when I was 16, and like many a young person engaging in a self-destructive habit, I felt it necessary to hide this aspect of my life from my parents and any other adult who might try to thwart me.

At first I told no blatant lies—I simply omitted the information. But as time went on and I was confronted with direct questions, I responded by telling direct fibs.

The woman at the grocery store, for instance, told my mother I'd tried to buy cigarettes. "They were for this kid," I explained. "I just wanted to see if I looked 18."

As I got older and started driving my own car, my dad would sometimes comment on the smell. Other times he'd confront me with loose cigarettes that had fallen from my handbag and landed under the passenger seat. "Oh, that," I'd say. "It must belong to Jerry. I gave him a ride the other day."

During my third year of college I was home for the weekend and was sitting at the table eating a satsuma. (Ever since I can remember, I have always peeled my satsumas the same way—so that the peel, in the end, looks like an elephant [ears, trunk].) My father walked into the house and, without a word, placed a photograph on the table in front of me.

That's right: the photo was one of me dangling a cigarette between my index and middle fingers. I'd left it in the glove box by accident, and my dad happened upon it while cleaning my car. In a split second I formulated all kinds of lies. I was holding it for a friend—that Jerry again. Yeah, that's Sarah—she does bear a striking resemblance to me, doesn't she? But there is a point at which the game is up—and I quickly realized this was it. My dad, you see, was in tears. I'd seen him shed a tear only once before, and that was at a funeral—so this rattled me.

My father had believed my stories—even when they'd stretched the boundaries of credulity, he'd had faith that I was telling the truth.

I hadn't considered how lying to someone you love is the worst sort of betrayal. All I'd thought about was how I didn't want to get in trouble. Of course my dad forgave me, as he always does, but that doesn't stop me feeling rotten about it—even after all these years. But Dad, here's my compliment to you: You make me want to be a better woman.

TO QUIT A bad habit—to change—you need proper motivation. I'm not convinced that "concepts" or "ideas" qualify. They are often rational and sensible and true, but I'm not convinced anyone ever changes for an idea. You'll change for a person, though. I quit smoking that same day my dad found the photograph—and in doing so I believe I became a better person. Not just a healthier person, or a better-smelling person, or a person able to run without wheezing, but a better person in the purest sense. There is only one way to become better, and it has nothing to do with the diameter of your thighs or how many certificates you have hanging on your wall or your latest promotion at work or your macrobiotic diet.

If you want to be better, you have to live up to the faith people have in you. You have to do the right things. "It can be so hard to know what the right thing is," people will tell you. Maybe if you're a turnip. Otherwise, it's remarkably easy to know what's right. Ain't always easy to do it—but trying to act as if a particular issue is "complicated" doesn't make it so.

Alcoholics Anonymous advises its members to take life "one day at a time." This is good advice for everyone. Just for today, tell yourself that you will not do anything you have to lie about. Just for today, be better by being less of an individual and more of a part of your family and community. Remind yourself, anytime you're tempted to think of your life as "complicated," that this is a word for people seeking to avoid accountability.

A life of honesty and integrity, a life spent thinking more about your obligations than about your "rights," is not easy—but it is simple.

SEARCHING FOR
THE SUMMIT

WHEN PEOPLE ASK how my mountain climb was, I always say, "Fun!"
Some people accept this at face value. These are people with only the vaguest
notion of what a "mountain" is. Anyone else raises an eyebrow—skeptical.
I can't tell you how many of my friends suspect that I am in the throes of a
midlife crisis.

"OK," I admit, defeated. "It was a *very particular kind* of fun."

"Like not fun?" said my brother—who has been up a mountain or two
in his day.

"That all depends on what the word *fun* means."

"Hey," he said. "Don't go all Bill Clinton on me."

THERE ARE MANY routes up Mount Rainier. We went via Camp Muir
and the Disappointment Cleaver over the course of three days. On Sunday
we set out early from Paradise—a popular viewing spot for tourists and the
location of the ranger station—after presenting our permits and registering
our itinerary. In order to keep traffic on the mountain at a reasonable level,
climbing parties must apply for a permit at the beginning of the season, list-
ing preferred days. Even if you do get the dates you want, the weather may
be unsuitable. July is the best month for climbing, but because of schedule
conflicts among various members of our group, we chose a couple of days
in late June. Lucky for us, this turned out to be one of the best runs of
weather on the mountain in recent years.

"This is *the* weekend, baby!" the guys at Marmot—a mountaineering
outfitter where my dad and I rented crampons and boots—enthused. "You're
doing the DC? Yeah, the route's kickin'. Just ride right on up the back of the
Cleaver, hop on the Emmons, and you're golden."

I'd already done a "dress rehearsal" up to Camp Muir (10,200 feet) four
days before the real thing—to check my conditioning and help increase my

tolerance to the altitude. The climb to Camp Muir, while not dangerous or technical, does involve a vertical ascent of almost 5,000 feet and can take anywhere from five to seven hours. With a heavy pack on your back and the unrelenting glare of the sun beating down on your back and bouncing up off the snow, trust me: you don't "ride" up anything. There is no "hopping." You trudge, one step at a time, over a long, steep, and endless snowfield. If you're lucky, you find a long chain of steps someone else kicked into the snow, and you—quite literally—follow in their footsteps.

Back from my dress rehearsal on Muir, near the car park, my dad and I bumped into a couple of tourists. "You've been to Muir?" they asked admiringly. I couldn't wait until Sunday, when I'd set out with my full pack—a sure sign to other hikers that you're one of those "headed all the way up." As much as possible, I like to impress people. Unfortunately, I rarely succeed.

Looking all cool is what kept me going Sunday—groaning under the weight of my pack. During the dress rehearsal run up Muir, I'd laughed and talked so much that I sunburned the tip of my tongue. When the real deal came, I spoke very little. It took all my energy to keep putting one foot in front of the other—and to smile at fellow hikers who'd say, "Going all the way up?"

I reckoned this first day would be the most difficult because of our heavy packs. Monday would be a short day. We'd rope up and cross the Cowlitz Glacier and over the Cathedral Rocks to the Ingraham Flats, where we'd set up camp for a short "night"—rising at 11:00 p.m. to start our final ascent to the summit. Tuesday morning, if all went according to plan, we'd make the summit—with light packs—then head back to the campsite, break camp, and hightail it down to the car. The packs would still be heavy, but we'd be going downhill.

"So was the first day the most difficult?" my brother asked.

"Depends on what you mean by most difficult."

"This conversation," he said, "is starting to bore me."

ON ONE OF the first hikes I did with my dad, when I was about 8 years old, he locked the keys in the car. Dad is famous for this: also, for losing things. We all laugh about it and would probably worry that it signaled some sort of old-age decline, but he's always been like this. I'm sorry to report he shows no signs of improving.

That first night at Camp Muir the tents were pitched, the gas fires were busy melting water, and Dan Wysong—who has far too much energy for my comfort—was sitting up at the top of a huge crumbling rock formation. My dad, rifling through his pack, suddenly said, "I can't find the suppers!"

"Don't be ridiculous," I said. "You packed and repacked those suppers 17 times." And even as the words left my mouth, I knew we were doomed. Not only had Dad left our packets of noodles and rice sitting in the back of his Highlander; he'd also forgotten the hot cider and half the packets of hot chocolate. Earlier that day we'd opened our lunches to find our peanut butter sandwiches blue with mold.

We sheepishly accepted spicy beans and rice from Dan and a pack of noodles that Chuck Davis generously offered, and we went to sleep pleasantly full.

The next morning I was in the tent sipping a mug of runny porridge when I noticed Dad sifting frantically through both his pack and mine. "I can't find my harness!" he said. "I pulled both the harnesses out last night and put them in the tops of the packs so they'd be easy to find. What am I going to do? Maybe I can just tie a rope around my waist like we used to back in the old days."

My husband is also like my dad: neither of them knows how to look. When Japhet loses his keys, he stands in the middle of the room and scans it. "They aren't here!" he shouts. Sometimes I take pity on him and start lifting things. Invariably the keys are cradled under a sofa cushion or hidden by a stray sock. I let Dad sweat for a few more minutes, then I slipped on my boots and stepped out into the snow. "What's this?" I said after about 10 seconds, dangling the harness in his face.

"Don't you know the rules?" my brother asked. "Never—I mean, *never*—let Dad pack."

WE WERE AT our second campsite, on the Ingraham Glacier, from before noon until just before midnight on Monday. We built a wall of snow bricks—like an igloo—to shield our tents from the wind. We spent hours melting snow and filling our water bottles. Actually, it would be more accurate to say that the three men built both the igloo and melted all the snow. I sat in my tent and read *The Clan of the Cave Bear*, poking my head out every once in a while to see how it was all going.

Chuck put Dan down a crevasse so he could prussick out. Prussicks are looped ropes tied with a special knot to your main rope. They enable you to climb out of a crevasse if you should fall in. On the one hand, I thought going into a crevasse sounded like fun—but on the other hand, I didn't want to do anything that might use up what little energy I had. I'd already practiced my prussicks hanging by my waist from a beam in my dad's garage. I took the same approach as when Dad told me to practice falling down a hill upside down and backwards and trying to self-arrest. "Nah," I said. "I'm doing that only if I have to."

We went to bed early, as soon as it started getting cold. It was hard for any of us to sleep, but we needed to rest before the final ascent. "Good to be horizontal," Chuck said.

"What do you think the chances are that, while we're sleeping, a crevasse will open under us and swallow our tents?" I asked—always thinking of worst-case scenarios. This is what I do for fun.

"You've got a better chance of winning the lottery," Dan said.

Chuck's alarm beeped at 11:00 p.m. None of us had slept much—certainly not soundly. We used the light from our headlamps to get dressed. We carried extra clothes, water, and food in our packs.

I wore long underwear, snow trousers, a harness, boots, crampons, a shirt, a fleece, a woolly hat, and a helmet. In my pack I carried a down coat, a waterproof shell, and two pairs of gloves. I also had packs of a high-energy "food" made of brown rice sugar and available in a "variety of flavors" that all taste of bitter honey. I also carried sunglasses for the descent, a pocketknife, two liters of Gatorade, and a Ziploc bag filled with peanuts, M&Ms, raisins, and broken crisps.

Halfway across the Ingraham Glacier, I felt something sharp in my boot. A small rock. It was too much trouble to remove it, and anyway, it shifted, so most of the time I couldn't feel it. It traveled with me all the way to the summit.

"Not only did I climb Mount Rainier, but I did it with a rock in my boot!" I boasted to my brother.

"Aren't you the tough cookie," he said.

A CLEAVER IS a huge rock formation that separates two glaciers—in the case of the Disappointment Cleaver, it separates the Ingraham and Emmons.

"Why 'Disappointment'?" I asked Chuck Davis—who reached the summit of Rainier for the third time on this trip.

"'Cause people would get to the top of the Cleaver and realize they were still almost 2,000 feet from the summit," Chuck said. "Pretty disappointing."

By the time we reached the top of the Cleaver (12,300 feet), I understood the name all too well. Up until then, anytime my companions asked how I was doing, I'd respond with a cheery "Still got my happy thoughts!" and I was mostly telling the truth. But on the final ascent, just before sunrise, I struggled to remember what the word "happy" meant. My legs burned. I was thirsty, a little queasy. My head felt strangely heavy. I found myself reaching far into my mind, trying to find games I could play to make the physical struggle easier.

"When you feel bad, smile!" I remembered reading somewhere. According to the experts, the physical act of smiling lifts your mood. So I started grinning like a maniac. This felt so ridiculous that within a few minutes I was giggling uncontrollably. It's lucky I was roped 40 feet from any of my companions, otherwise the cackling might have made them nervous. I was, after all, thirsty, oxygen-deprived, and carrying an ice axe.

It is the middle of the night, I thought. *I should be sleeping. I'm on the side of a mountain. Way up high. I could lose my balance. If I do, I could bring everyone down with me. Don't fall. Hey, I wonder if those lights in the far distance are Yakima! Oh, dear God, please don't leave me. Why, oh, why did I come here? I'm going to die. Hee-hee-hee-hee-hee. This is hysterical!*

"What's fun about that?" a friend asked.

"It was a very particular kind of fun," I said, knowing I'd probably never be able to explain it, except perhaps to a kindred spirit.

ON A MOUNTAIN, as in life, there comes a point—somewhere in the middle of the final ascent—where you lose the plot. You have only the foggiest recollection of the choices that brought you this far. It is dark. Your life is a pinpoint. You lack perspective. You're without faith. All your choices seem suspect. Why, you wonder, did I pack peanuts as a snack? If I had it to do over, I'd take Doritos.

"If you'd brought Doritos," the logic center of your brain counters, "right now you'd hate them, too. Accept it: There's nothing you could have done to preempt this moment. It was ordained from the beginning; rearrange the variables any way you want. No matter what, right now you'd want to do it all differently."

I'll call it a midmountain crisis. Very similar to a midlife crisis, but without the sports cars and tummy tucks. There's just the tightness in your gut, a feeling of impending doom, the realization that it all hangs on you—no safety net—and the sickening suspicion that you are not up to the task. People are depending on you. What if you fail them?

"Quit," a little voice in your head whispers seductively.

"No," you say.

"QUIT!" it screams.

"NO!" And as if to underscore your determination, you squeeze a packet of brown rice sugar pure energy "food" into your mouth and swallow with a grimace.

"Now leave me alone," you say calmly. "Let me put this baby to bed."

THE SUN RISES. A bright ball against the curve of the earth. Crisis averted. You have an aha moment. "Aha!" you say. "That's why people do this."

You can see the curve of the earth. It feels as if the whole world has unfurled itself before you. I began to weep at the site of the world. *It's so big,* I thought. *Why did I never know the world was so big?*

I know what you're thinking: if I could see the curve of the earth, that means it's small. But that isn't how it seemed. From high on the mountain, everything seemed possible. It seemed likely, even, that in such a big world there might even be a place for someone like me.

I plunged forward, almost crawling, leaning heavily on my ice axe with both hands. Time passed. I had crazy, oxygen-deprived thoughts. Then Chuck and Dan were taking off their ropes ahead of me. "What's going on?" I shouted, fearful of what this might mean.

Chuck pointed. "We can walk the rest of the way unroped." We were at the crater—in sight of the summit.

Chuck and Dan went ahead while I unroped and walked over to my dad. One of his gloves had blown down the mountain during a water break and his hand was frozen: purple, stiff, and clawlike.

"You go," he growled. "I'm not going all the way over there. Been there, done it. This is far enough."

He never would have let me get away with that—and I didn't let him.

"Stuff that," I said. "It's not even 6:00 in the morning. We're ahead of schedule. Stop being such a grouch."

So we set off together across the crater, watching steam rise from cracks in the volcano. I signed the book tucked inside a steel box chained to a rock, and the four of us took pictures.

And for a few minutes, before we had to start worrying about the descent (where, incidentally, you're most likely to have an accident), it was fun in the purest sense. We were at the top. We hadn't fallen victim to acute mountain sickness or pulmonary edema. We hadn't fallen in a crevasse or dragged each other, flailing and helpless, off the end of the DC. For at least a few moments the struggle was over. Mission accomplished.

I've so rarely been at the top of anything. And in "life," unlike mountaineering, the top is a subjective, elusive thing. How do you know when you're there? There's no altimeter to let you know how much higher. There's no steel box where you can add your name to the long list of others who have come before you. There's nothing but an endless snowfield and crazy footprints going in all directions. You wander and pray and hope for the best. Hope that you end up somewhere. Hope that you don't fall or drag anyone else down with you.

"You *are* having a midlife crisis!" one of my friends said triumphantly.

"Every day for the past 20 years," I said. "No biggie."

ON THE WAY down we passed a large guided group headed up. One of the women smiled at me. "Congratulations," she said.

"Congratulations, you!" I answered. "You're as good as there."

"How much farther?" the man behind her asked, gasping for air. "Ten minutes?"

"Sure," I answered.

"Good," he said. "I can *do* 10."

I smiled to myself as we carried on down. *Buddy*, I thought, *if it were 20, you could do 20, and if it were an hour, I believe you'd still be huffing along.* That's the best thing we humans have going for us: we persevere. Most of the time we even manage a smile, a grim joke. Whether we ever make it or not, we're always searching for the summit. Humanity, that's why I love you.

"Huh," my brother said. "You wouldn't be going all deep and philosophical if it was *really* fun."

SO REFRESHING

IT WAS MY eighth flight in a little more than two weeks, and I was tired of everything relating to aviation. Stuffy air. Unappealing films. Food encased in foil and shrink-wrapped plastic. Announcements over the intercom system—sometimes (and always twice as long) in French. The Fasten Your Seat Belt sign. Small cans of fizzy drink. Polyester flight socks.

In summary: flying stinks.

"But flight is a miracle of the modern world," you say. "Just think, 200 years ago our ancestors would probably never have made such a trip, and if they did, it would have been first in the hull of a ship, vomiting, and then perhaps in a covered wagon or stagecoach, being alternately robbed by Jesse James and set upon by the few hostile Indians who were still alive after being intentionally infected with measles, mumps, and rubella and succumbing to the diseases because of the less than 70 percent uptake of the MMR vaccine among Native Americans fearful of becoming like Dustin Hoffman in *Rainman*."

Meh. Don't know. Just not feeling it. You know all those people from the old days whom everyone pities, the ones who never traveled more than 10 miles from where they were born in their whole lives? Maybe I envy them a little. I am tired of removing my shoes, showing my passport, and stating whether I am on business or pleasure. I'm tired of agricultural beagles sniffing my suitcase and watching videos explaining how the oxygen mask system works while thinking, *I'm never going to remember this.* Sometimes I am tired of London. Does this really mean I'm tired of life?

Chicago's O'Hare Airport did not even have a Starbucks in the international terminal. My throat was scratchy. I had a headache. The only thing keeping me from banging my head on the industrial carpet tiles of the airport lounge during my three-hour wait was an excellent book of essays on slightly bizarre topics. That and an unreasoning fear of drawing unwarranted attention to myself—and being, perhaps, asked to remove my shoes yet again.

There seems to be some sort of natural law in place that dictates that if you are in a bad mood, you will immediately be placed in close proximity to people who are so perky you suspect them of crack cocaine use.

Of course, that's what happened to me. When I boarded my next flight, there were three teenage girls next to me in the four-seat middle section of the 747, and they were bouncing up and down with joy. They were so happy to be on an airplane. Everything fascinated them—the Duty Free catalog, the headphones. "Aren't these small cans cute?" they enthused when the beverage cart came round, causing me to roll my eyes so far back I momentarily lost consciousness. For a while, after resisting the impulse to inquire as to whether any or all of them suffered from ADHD, I simply blocked their conversation out as best I could, smirking every so often at a remark I couldn't help overhearing: "Wow, socks!" or "This is the tiniest, sweetest toothpaste tube I've ever seen!"

After a "supper" of small, cute items, the lights went out for the movies and for sleep time. I wanted to continue reading my book, so I flipped my overhead light on. "How'd that happen?" the girls exclaimed. "How'd that light come on? Didja touch sumpthin'?"

"It was me," I said. "You see this little button with the lightbulb icon? That turns on your overhead light. If you'd like me to start at the very beginning (a very good place to start), once upon a time there was a very tenacious man called Thomas Edison. And before Edison, Benjamin Franklin went kite flying and harnessed the power of something we earthlings like to call 'electricity.' "

This was enough to convince the girls that I was an expert at air travel—which, oddly enough, cheered me up. I am so rarely regarded as an expert at anything that this kind of deference made me feel almost successful, as if I should be wearing a power suit and shouting into a mobile phone.

They then asked my advice on everything. "Do you think, ma'am, that I can climb up over the back of the seat to get to the restroom—or is that not allowed?" the girl next to me asked nervously. My pleasure at being an aviation expert was tempered only by the girl's reflexive use of "ma'am." Some people may consider this form of address polite, but it makes me feel as though I must surely have puffy blue hair and a colostomy bag.

"Hey," I said, "I'm thinking so long as you don't try to stab anyone with a plastic fork, you're probably good."

"This is our first time on an airplane," the girl finally confessed. "Well, today anyway. The flight from Georgia to Chicago this morning was technically the very first."

It seems obvious now, but at the time it had not occurred to me that the girls were unfamiliar with airplanes. I thought they were just stupid. And why did I think they were stupid? Because anyone over the age of 9 who doesn't know better than to curb their enthusiasm in a public place is obviously a few chromosomes short of a . . . uh, complete set of chromosomes.

"You've never been on an airplane?" I asked, incredulous.

"No, ma'am," the girl said. "Well, one of those itty-bitty ones with, like, two seats. But nuthin' like this!"

The girls soon hunkered down to watch a movie starring Matthew McConaughey, and I was left in the dark with my thoughts. Mostly I began to wonder when the last time was that I felt excited about something. I couldn't remember. I approach most endeavors with something like low-level dread. And it's hard to get excited when you keep getting that feeling that you've seen it all before.

I don't remember exactly when I stopped feeling uninhibited joy, but maybe it was around the same time I stopped expressing it.

I do remember the moment I realized I would never be shocked by anything again. That was the time I turned on the television just in time to see the second plane crash into the World Trade Center in New York. Perhaps an hour later both buildings collapsed with a tremendous dusty sigh. I sat back on the sofa and exhaled and thought: *Mark this moment and remember how it feels, because this is the last time you will ever be shocked. And you're only 29.*

For the most part, I was right. I've felt sadness—at the tsunami, the summer of beheadings in Iraq, the hurricane in New Orleans, the London bombings last year, etc.—but none of it sucker-punched me. It wasn't that I was expecting disaster—it's more that I wasn't not expecting it. Every day I pull up *The Times Online* and read the headlines, expecting anything. In December of 2005, when the Buncefield oil depot blew up three miles from my house in Hemel Hempstead, I peered out the window at the enormous column of black smoke rising a mile into the sky and thought (before I'd seen the news), *London is gone*, and even then I didn't feel especially surprised.

MY HUSBAND LIKES action movies. I don't. My typical summing up of such films on walking past the snack corner on the way to the car park is

"Too many explosions." This is also perhaps the greatest criticism I could offer of the world today. Too many explosions. Cheap predictable plot. An overreliance on special effects. Does the world have to be both tragic and boring? Somebody, please, surprise me. Play against type. Blow me away. I want to be gobsmacked. What I want is to feel delight, but I am no longer sure that's possible.

Is this what it means to be jaded? Is this why the three Southern girls chose to call me ma'am—because of the world-weariness I carry around me like a moth-eaten shawl? And once you get jaded, how do you go back? Is there a point of no return—a rickety bridge that collapses in a dusty heap as soon as you step onto the other side of a great chasm, leaving you forever cut off from the person you once were?

THE FIRST TIME I flew on an airplane, I was 8 years old. My family went to Maui on holiday. Yes, I was excited about flying—but back in the late seventies everything was exciting. For fun we used to go to the airport to watch the planes take off. For fun we'd go through the metal detectors. This is what we did for fun. In the late seventies I would have been delighted if anyone had asked me to remove my shoes.

What's the difference between then and now? Why do I no longer cartwheel through security? Well, partly because my hamstrings couldn't take it. But also because since I was 8 I've done a lot of flying. It's become old hat. I don't think I could get excited about an airplane if I tried. I want a new hat. One with lots of sequins. You can't manufacture excitement where none exists. Can you?

Why, then, are Christians always trying? Why is it when you go to church, invariably someone stands up and shouts, "Isn't the Bible exciting?" or "It's time to get excited about Jesus!"

If you aren't "passionate" about Christ, the church, salvation, etc., the general consensus is that there is something wrong with you and with your spiritual life. You are supposed to do something to pump yourself up. Go on a mission trip. Attend a "crusade." Witness in a frenzied and manic way.

Isn't it reasonable to assume that once a person knows the drill—once they've experienced a given activity countless times—they'll become, if not bored exactly, perhaps something like low-key? Is there anything wrong with low-key?

"Low-key people don't tend to accomplish much," you say.

True. But you know those excited girls on the airplane? They got to London. So did I. They bounced off the plane while I dragged my sorry, miserable self onto the moving walkway, but the point is, I arrived. Without being happy or excited.

Put that in your pipe.

"DON'T WAFFLE SO much," my writing teacher in high school used to scribble on my essays. "Make a point and stick to it."

It's good advice, Mrs. Z, and I wish I could take it. It's just that I'm the kind of person who likes to wander around the perimeter slowly, checking for flaws, poking for weaknesses. The kind of person who makes a point and sticks to it is the sort who never wonders what a thing would look like if you were to turn it around. Or upside down. If you were to jump up and down on it for 10 minutes in your heavy boots.

I hold the following truths to be self-evident:

1. Excitement cannot be manufactured.

2. Experience tends to dull your zest for things like small cans and also things like sermons.

3. Your feelings aren't that important. But:

4. Feeling good is nice.

As a moody person, I have to remind myself of number 3 a lot. Every day. My life can't be about how I feel. I can't rate the quality of my career, my relationships, or anything else based on how I feel about them, because that changes like clockwork, like the lineup of that eighties Latino band Menudo.

Even so, shall I tell you how I really felt about the three Southern girls on my flight from Chicago to London? After the initial shock of them wore off, they charmed me. Utterly and completely. Their simple excitement and guilelessness were refreshing and sweet. It pleased me. The emperor was pleased.

Excitement doesn't necessarily mean anything, but you know what? It *is* more fun.

Perhaps you can never go back to feeling what you did when you first found Christ or first put on a pair of polyester airline socks, but you can at least be happy for others. You can remember that you were once the way they are now. Life flows and changes, and you change with it, but perhaps the best way to avoid becoming jaded—especially about church—is to spend time with people for whom the whole experience is fresh and exciting.

I have a confession: those small airplane cans of soda are pretty wicked.

FRIES WITH THAT

AFTER MY FIRST year at college, I began searching for a summer job. My parents correctly believed that I would value my education more if I had a hand in paying for it, and so they set a modest sum that I would need to raise by the end of my summer break.

Being, as I was, a veteran of one whole year of college, and having aced such courses as Criminology, United States History, and Psychology 101, I thought I'd have no problem procuring an easy job in a clean, air-conditioned environment. I hoped for employment at a trendy boutique where I'd be primarily required to wear cute clothes and occasionally give off a sophisticated, tinkling laugh to no one in particular.

I don't remember now just how many jobs I applied for—traipsing through the local shopping mall in high heels and carrying my Gucci bag to signal the quality of my taste to potential employers. What I do remember is how distinctly unimpressed everyone seemed to be with my qualifications—which, it must be noted, were nonexistent. At that point, I'd held the following jobs: dining room assistant at a German retirement home, babysitter, janitor (specializing in men's toilets), day-care assistant teacher (fancy term for "diaper changer"), and photocopier for the department of history and political science.

"Do you have any retail experience?" these mall clowns kept asking, and I couldn't figure out what *experience* had to do with anything. I mean, seriously, people, I got an "A–" in World Geography. Ask me anything about major bodies of water or mountain ranges. I can tell you the capital of any country in the world, right here, right now. Just ask me.

"What's the capital of the country formerly known as East Pakistan?" you ask.

And the answer to that is as follows: I'll have to get back to you. In just a tick.

"Googling's cheating," you say.

I'm not going to Google it. I'm going to, as Hercule Poirot might say, use my leetle gray cells. Everything you've ever learned is in your brain somewhere. You just have to coax it out. And when coaxing fails, I've always found banging my head repeatedly against a bamboo floor extremely effective. The floor, though, has to be bamboo. With cheap laminate, well, you get what you pay for.

ABOUT A WEEK passed, and I still didn't have a job. My brother, who had just turned 16, found a job before I did, at McDonald's. No way did I want to work in any kind of fast-food establishment. I was far too good for that. "I've been to college," I said. "No way I'm working a McJob with a bunch of losers and retards."

Famous last words. My advice to you? Never sneer at a situation unless you happen to want to be transported straight into it, in a puff of green smoke. And this can't be tricked. You can't, for instance, try sneering at high-flying jobs at Microsoft as a way of tricking fate into giving you one. Fate may be slow, but it ain't stupid.

"Tick-tock," my dad said. "Time's wasting. That money isn't going to magically appear under your pillow, you know."

Wendy's Old Fashioned Hamburgers had a huge, frightening "Now Hiring" sign in the window. Crushed and demoralized, I decided to lower myself to this terrible level and went inside to fill out an application. To my horror, even Wendy's wasn't overjoyed at the prospect of hiring me.

"What do you know about french fries?" the nervous assistant manager who hired me asked.

"They're greasy and they make you fat and pimply," I answered, tossing my hair in disdain.

"Know how to add?" he asked.

"Of course I know how to add," I said, offended. "Didn't I mention I'm a college student?"

"Worst adders in the world," he said. "What's $46.27 plus $18.92?"

"Uhhhh . . ." I said.

He smiled, triumphant. "I guess we'll have to start you on drinks. You can pick up your shirt and visor tomorrow at the start of your shift. You'll need your own trousers—either navy blue or black. And a pair of slip-proof shoes. Welcome to Wendy's."

The general manager came over to welcome me too. "This job involves a lot of hustling," he said. "Know how to hustle?"

I was unsure of precisely what he meant. "Hustle," after all, has a variety of meanings. But I sensed the correct answer was yes.

I tried to cover my discomfort with a wan smile. "Sure," I said. "I can hustle."

FIRST I LEARNED drinks, then fries, then sandwiches. After one week I started on the front register. Although I'd done my share of low-skilled jobs in the past, they had always been somewhat behind the scenes. Crowds do not generally assemble, for instance, to watch you scrub caked urine from the bathroom walls, entertaining as that may be.

At Wendy's Old Fashioned Hamburgers, smack in the middle of Bellevue, Washington's business district, people lined up 50 deep during the daily lunch rush that generally lasted about two hours. Most of them had little to do while they waited, so they made use of their time by staring at me in a lazy but nevertheless intimidating fashion.

The fast-food industry is all about the psychology of degradation. "They" want to make sure you never feel even a fraction of the self-esteem necessary to search out a better job. Not only was my horizontally striped golf shirt an unflattering teal and gray, but I was forced to wear a polyester visor scrunched down over my brow, giving me a *Clan of the Cave Bear* look. The official excuse was that the visor serves as a hygiene instrument—keeps your hair from falling in the food. But most of the managers also had hair. None of them wore visors—nor the dreaded teal golf shirts.

When you look hideous, it is very difficult to maintain an attitude of quiet confidence and good cheer. This difficulty is compounded when people treat you with contempt, as if you are a lower life form, when they speak slowly to you, as if they believe that you are mentally deficient. How do you keep from crumbling emotionally when everyone you see, all day long, is better than you? Dressed better with good jobs and nice cars. Spoiled customers your own age socialize in tight contemptuous clusters, and you're sure they're giggling about you. Even postal employees look down their noses. It isn't hard to see why the average person finds the prospect of this type of employment almost unbearably depressing.

But here's the thing: few things are ever as bad as you imagine them to be. Being drawn and quartered might be. But other things—those that do not involve violent death—are usually much more hideous in your mind. The trip to the dentist. Doing your taxes. Taking a driving test. Saying to strangers, 800 times a day, "Would you like fries with that?" and cringing when they respond with a sarcastic and pointed "Did I ask for fries? Then *no fries, retard."*

If you are one of those people who prefers to warm your parents' settee and sleep till noon rather than take a job that's "beneath" you, I'd highly recommend that you go out today and take the first thing coming. It's like boot camp—horrible, painful—but you come out the other side a slightly better you. And come on: most of these jobs are so horrible, they're downright amusing.

During my first week at Wendy's this insane fellow employee freaked out when I touched the fries. "Don't touch my fries!" she shrieked, her eyes rolling in her head like one of those seizing patients on the TV show *House.* "If you touch my fries, I'll kill you."

At first I was shocked. Then I couldn't help it: I started to laugh. Fifteen years later it still cracks me up. And that's hardly the most amusing of my fast-food anecdotes. I worked at Wendy's four summers and most Christmas holidays, too. What a lot of freaks and weirdos I met along the way. Psychology 101 is perfectly useful, but there's nothing like a bird's-eye view of how people behave when no one who matters is watching. That's how you can see what a person is truly made of. And in watching other people, you start to learn a little bit about that ultimate weirdo stranger—yourself.

ALMOST EVERYONE I know, me included, would say they want a job that is "meaningful." I've thought for some time about what this really means, as I've long suspected it is, in fact, a kind of code. Try replacing the word "meaningful" with the word "prestigious." Now we're getting somewhere. Because rarely is any kind of work all that odious—particularly if it impresses other people. That takes the sting right out, better than an ice cube.

Take the Peace Corps, for instance. If you worked for the Peace Corps, you might well end up managing some kind of raw sewage. But managing sewage for the Peace Corps would be widely regarded as more "meaningful"—and therefore more prestigious—than if you worked in sewage at, say, Dacorum Borough Council. People are people and sewage is sewage and it all smells bad—but the admiring looks you get when you tell people you are with the Peace Corps? Priceless.

NOT ABSOLUTELY SURE this is true, and unfortunately, I lack the large-scale facilities—not to mention the salivating dogs—necessary to conduct a full-scale psychological investigation, so, as per usual, I'll use my intuition: I betcha that if working fast-food paid six figures and was well-esteemed, it would feel a lot more meaningful.

But what is "meaning"? And what matters? Take an individual doing a job that most would agree is meaningful, such as a doctor. So what if he or she saves lives? Everybody dies someday anyway. Maybe by saving a life you're actually doing that patient a disservice. Maybe you're serving that person up to a far more painful death 10 years down the road.

"You're completely demented," my brother said when I ran this point of view by him.

But I don't, by any means, believe that nothing matters. I'm just messing with you. Quite the contrary: I believe everything matters.

"Whether I use butter or margarine?" you ask.

Everything. Not everything equally, mind you. Some things matter far more than margarine—but nothing is inconsequential. What you do, how you think, your irritating little habits and flaws, whether you take pride in your work—these all come together and make you who you are. Who you are is the second most important thing in the whole world. The first most important is cheese.

Kidding. The first most important, of course, is who Jesus is. Jesus is, without any doubt, the one who makes you matter. And Jesus loves you. But don't think that's an excuse for sitting on your parents' settee and refusing to work because all the available jobs are too lowly for the likes of you.

DOING MEANINGFUL WORK that uses your talents is great. If it impresses other people and boosts your flagging ego, all the better. But what we all need to get used to is the idea of taking a given task seriously—no matter how lowly or degrading it may seem.

Just this week I saw the film *Johnny English* with my 6-year-old son. Those of you who've seen it may remember that the title character, played by Rowan Atkinson, spends most of his time fantasizing about being a suave Bondlike character. So intent is Johnny on being the hero, the "big man," that he doesn't pay attention to "petty" details, like doing his job. Within the first five minutes of the movie all the agents in England are killed because of Johnny's inability to accept his unglamorous position as a support worker with the British Secret Service.

Do you ever find yourself acting a bit like this? Ever wish you were more important than you are? Do you slouch off on the tasks your boss wants you to do while spending most of your time complaining that your talents are going unrecognized? Do you refuse to do tasks that are boring or embarrassing? If so, I hate to break this to you, but you'll never get anywhere in life.

If you want more responsibility and more "meaning" in your working life, follow these three rules: 1. Be punctual and neatly dressed. 2. Do any duty assigned you to the best of your ability without whining, making faces, or attempting to pass the work off to someone else. If possible, do your work with cheer and good humor. This applies even when the task involves mopping up an overflowing toilet. 3. Accept criticism with grace and learn from it—even when you feel it's unjustified. Especially when you feel it's unjustified.

You can always learn—even if it's something as simple as how to be humble without thinking of yourself as a loser. It's a fine balance.

And may I remind you, Jesus did not find any task beneath Himself while on this earth. He could've gotten a big head about His heavenly mission and refused to work in the carpenter shop, a lowly trade. He could've blown off God's calling to minister to the poor and needy. But He accepted every challenge and every task with an untiring spirit.

YOU'VE NO DOUBT been holding your breath in anticipation. Drum roll. East Pakistan is the former name for the country now known as Bangladesh. The capital is Dhaka. Rhymes with "soccer." Probably.

"I've never met anyone who spends more time thinking about useless rubbish than you do," a good friend told me recently.

I blushed furiously, unable to contain my pleasure at such a fine and unexpected compliment.

"Shucks," I said. "Thanks!"

FOR THOSE ABOUT
TO ROCK

THE PRESENTER SHOWED slides. Dozens of slides on a big white screen, the kind you pull up from the floor and hook into a frame. He brought a laser pointer so he could shine a bright-red dot on all the things we teenagers might tend to overlook. We were blinded, he said, seduced by forces we couldn't begin to understand. The presenter sweated and wiped his brow with a cotton cloth. His tie had a spot of grease, just above one of the fat blue horizontal stripes.

The first slide contained the title of the presentation in black-and-red hand-drawn fancy letters: "For Those About to Rock." And in smaller writing beneath: "Could your favorite songs be the product of satanic forces?"

This was not our first time at a presentation, not the first time we'd leaned back in our chairs and surveyed an adult stranger with a briefcase and visual aids hoping to teach us a thing or two about life. Being a young person is a bit like being the Hollywood Walk of Fame—everyone and their third cousin wants to leave their handprints on you. Footprints, too, if you'll let them. They hope to leave an imprint on your life. This is what they mean when they talk of "touching young people's lives." They hope you will never forget what they tell you. Sometimes they hold you by the chin, tight, so you can't look away, and they tell you something very important. "If you remember nothing else, remember this," they say, never seeming to realize that the average young person hears this about 38,000 times during the course of their upbringing, and each time it loses a bit of potency until it's like a tea bag that can't so much as turn the water amber.

Once we had an old man who came to school to show us slides he took of dinosaurs in the inky jungle of somewhere in centralish Africa. As per usual, these photos consisted mostly of black-and-white noise. "Look!" he'd say excitedly, pointing at a grayish blob on the screen. "There's the dinosaur's long neck!" He also had a laser pointer, and a tape deck that played the sound of a dinosaur roaring. This sounded almost exactly the way your car sounds when you're driving and you roll down all the windows on the highway. Still, he was a nice old man, and moreover, he was somebody's grandpa. We pretended to see and hear the dinosaurs. We gave a round of applause when he finished. And we were genuinely grateful to have escaped typing class with the dreaded "timed writings" that day.

The "For Those About to Rock" presenter was not anybody's grandpa. Moreover, he was interfering with a U.S. history class, a favorite during which our teacher would often walk around waving a pretend rifle and shouting—sometimes going so far as to leap onto his own desk.

My friend—and Advanced Foods cooking partner—Joey hissed at me from behind. "Psst," he said. "Five bucks says he brings up 'Hotel California.'"

"Emal ossi siht. Emal ossi siht," another guy said.

"Come again?" I said.

He slapped his leg and fell about in fits of laughter. "I'm backmasking," he said. "Dude, I'm like totally backmasking. Don't worry—it's all right there in your subconscious."

NOWADAYS, AMONG YOUNGER people, I doubt if there is any such thing as "rock" music. I have to admit I don't know the names of all the categories and subcategories. I know rap. I know jungle. Hip-hop? Disco? But back in the late eighties, it was all about the evils of rock music.

The evils of most things were a pretty easy sell for our teachers. To demonstrate the evils of alcohol, they took us to Children's Hospital in Seattle and wheeled out babies suffering from fetal alcohol syndrome. They had a "Smoking Sam" dummy to illustrate how smoking shrivels and destroys your lungs. Gruesome childbirth videos—complete with a close-up episiotomy—convinced us of the evils of sex at any life stage.

The evils of rock music are harder to pinpoint in terms of cause and effect. Many people listen to rock music without becoming alcoholics, committing suicide, or even having episiotomies. But . . . as every adult knows, there's something sinister about the loud, obnoxious stuff. The trick is working out just what it is.

For starters, rock music is obviously evil because it virtually always relies, to some extent, on a drumbeat. Drums have been known to be used in non-Christian African religious ceremonies in which chickens are sacrificed and all manner of debauchery takes place.

A teenager raises his hand. "But sir, wasn't much of modern Western music developed in a context of imperialism and colonization that deprived people around the world of their God-given freedom and dignity? Slavery and all that?"

The speaker, faced with having to make the dubious assertion that Africans are *more evil* than other people, switches gears. The African thing, he says, isn't the main point. The main point is that the devil was head musician in heaven. He knows a thing or two about music. That's why songs such as "Hotel California" are so appealing. It's so as to suck you in.

"But sir," the same teenager asks. "Doesn't that mean that the devil could have influenced Western classical music, too? And more specifically, church music, like the hymns we sing?"

"Backmasking!" the presenter shouts with growing desperation. "If you play certain rock songs backwards, they say things like 'I love Satan.'"

"Look at this album cover!" he cries. "Karen Carpenter is holding her hand in a clawlike pose, signifying a link with spiritualism."

The kids start to shuffle their feet restlessly. Is he talking about *Karen Carpenter?* The Carpenters, who sing "We've Only Just Begun" and "Rainy Days and Mondays"? He thinks she's a satanist? Dude.

The presenter flicks through his slides to one of an album cover featuring ice cubes. "If you look closely," he says, "you can see unmarried people lying in bed together. It's subliminal. Right there in the ice cubes. You kind of have to squint."

By now the kids are holding their index fingers close to their heads, making circular motions just above their ears in the universal symbol loosely translated as "He's nuts."

FOR AS LONG as people have walked the earth, they have fought, argued, gotten huffy, and occasionally wiped each other out over relatively trivial issues. The assassination of the Archduke Franz Ferdinand springs to mind. I mean seriously, who cares about that? No one I know. Of course, most of the people I know think Franz Ferdinand is a Glasgow-based rock band.

Then there are the really important things that people fight over—the sorts of things church people like ourselves bicker about ad nauseum. These include issues such as whether to present song lyrics on a screen via Microsoft PowerPoint, whether ties on the platform are optional, and whether a true Christian can make jokes. Not too long ago a woman became very angry with me because I offered her my left hand when she wanted to shake. My right arm was holding: (1) my squirmy toddler, (2) two raincoats and a jumper, and (3) a bag filled with nappies, snacks, and other Sabbath accessories. From my point of view, by offering my left—and, it must be noted, the only available—hand, I was making a gracious concession to good manners. Neither of us comes from cultures that have any particular negative connotations attached to the left hand. At least I don't think we do. Still, she managed to make an issue of it.

"Don't be offering me your left hand, girl," she snapped. Later she told my mother—not knowing who she was—that this was not a good church, that the people were not true Christians. Her evidence? A young woman offered her left hand to shake when a decent person would offer only her right.

My mother, long accustomed to complaints about me coming as regular as nuisance phone calls during evening tea, immediately suspected that I was the young woman in question. Laughing, she related my latest faux pas over Sabbath lunch. I immediately launched into a fit of self-loathing paranoia.

"Is there something about the left hand?" I asked. "I know there is in India, but what about here? Does everyone know except me?"

"Becky," my mom said, "the woman is crazy. Have pity."

"Maybe I'm crazy," I said.

My mother paused, took a bite of her potato, chewed thoughtfully, swallowed. "The woman is crazy too," she said.

I READ AN account of a cartoon recently that depicted Satan in hell, giving some newcomers a welcome tour. "You'll find there aren't many hard-and-fast rules here," he says. "Just whatever works for you."

Of course, this is a way of making fun of liberals—implying that the road to hell is paved with namby-pamby, morally relativistic, feel-good nonsense.

Funny thing is, if you turned that cartoon around and had God showing people around heaven and making the same statement—i.e., we don't have a lot of hard-and-fast rules here—that would totally jive for me, and for a lot of other people. I don't envision heaven as a place with "a lot" of rules. From what we know of the Garden of Eden, there appears to have been just the one: do not eat of the tree. This doesn't mean that I don't believe there is a difference between right and wrong—only that I think there are lots of ways to be right and lots of ways to be wrong.

THE ISSUE OF music in our church is widely considered so "contentious" that most people won't touch it with a stick. Think about that for a moment. Let it sink in. Music makes people so angry that they are rendered speechless. Seizures have been known to happen during all-church debates on the topic, especially if anyone mentions the timpani. Ambulances come screaming. Veins pop out of foreheads. Eyes bug out. Things get ugly. People will advise you not to talk about music. "If you value your skin," they'll say, shaking their heads.

Why?

I'm serious. If we're going to be vein-popping angry, why not blow a gasket about what's happening in Darfur? I don't have an answer. I'm asking you.

Por qué?

WHEN I GOT to be older—25, in fact—I was a youth leader, along with my husband, at a good-sized English church. A person I respect very much—who is also a well-schooled musician—suggested talking to the youth about music. The teenaged person inside me, the one who had witnessed "For Those About to Rock," cringed.

The man gave what I considered to be a pretty well-balanced argument. The gist of what he had to say is that music has an effect on you. An emotional effect. He cited the case of horror movies that rely on "scary" music to intensify the mood and create unbearable tension. He pointed out that scary music doesn't affect everyone "differently"—movie producers rely on the expectation that it will affect everyone in pretty much precisely the same way. Therefore, aggressive, angry music with a throbbing beat can't make you "happy," because it has an angry essence. And therefore you shouldn't listen to music with a heavy beat.

The kids, I noticed, were resistant to, even upset by, this argument. And even I, while agreeing with the broad strokes (of course music affects you—a butterfly flaps its wings in Tokyo, and it affects you), felt strangely unsettled by it. I wasn't sure why.

But I think I know why now. There is something flawed in this reasoning, something of a non sequitur. Not all people are affected in precisely the same way by music—or by anything. What do the words we use for emotions—"happy," "aggressive," "angry," "frightened"—even mean? It seems likely that we don't experience "happiness" in the same way. And scary music in movies scares me more than it does my husband. I am more susceptible, it would seem, to the mood-building suspense.

I've always been the same person, more or less. Recently, in a fit of nostalgia, I downloaded a song I used to love when I was 15. I stuck my iPod headphones in my ears and prepared to bop around the house with my Windex in hand, killing two birds with one stone. But I couldn't stand the song. It made me want to scream. If one person can react so differently to a musical piece because of the passage of time, isn't it conceivable that individuals also have varying responses?

More to the point: what, as Christians, is it appropriate for us to feel? Do we have to walk around in a vague fuzz of pleasant "happiness" all the time, or is there room for exploring other emotions, sometimes, perhaps, through music?

What really annoyed the kids in my youth group was the presumption that an adult, armed with "proof," should attempt to make them agree with his personal conclusion. They felt that if they accepted his basic assertion—that music affects you—they'd have to follow him down the path of listening to only what he fancies, what he thinks is nice.

Perhaps if we started imagining that our role in life is not to convince anyone of anything, but rather to be *holy*—not uptight or snooty, but holy—in all we do, we might start being angry about the right things and willing to withhold absolute judgment from time to time. That goes for all of us.

SIGN LANGUAGE

QUITE A FEW years ago, in a Paris restaurant, I went off in search of the bathroom. I followed the arrows until I came to the end of a corridor with two doors. Instead of the usual stick-person-with-a-skirt and stick-person-without-a-skirt that serve as universally recognized symbols of whether or not to anticipate a urinal, I found myself staring at two full-color murals, each covering one entire door.

The first: a hulking gorilla on a jungle backdrop eating a banana; the second: a large metal green snake with glittering eyes wrapped around the twisted trunk of a banyan tree.

I kept looking back and forth between the doors, certain there must be tiny writing indicating which one was "les femmes." I'm a pretty observant and freakishly thorough person. After about 60 seconds of looking, I concluded that the murals were the only clues I was going to get.

"It was like an intelligence test, and I was failing," I moaned to my friend Amy recently, breaking out in a nervous rash at the very thought of the murals. "Which is more like a woman: a gorilla or a snake?"

"Duh," Amy said. "The gorilla."

"Why?"

"Because it's a mammal."

"Men are mammals too, idiot."

"Oh. [Pause]. You sure?"

I am a character not unlike the sort Hugh Grant plays in movies—someone who takes a slightly awkward situation and makes it excruciating. I fidgeted and walked up and down the corridor trying to look nonchalant. I leaned against the wall, trying to decide what to do. Glancing at my watch, I took note of the time and decided that I would allow five minutes to pass. If, during those five minutes, no person of obvious sex persuasion exited either of the doors—thereby clueing me as to which one was mine—I would conclude that both bathrooms were most likely empty. Then I would flip a coin: heads being gorilla and tails being snake. According to the fate dealt me by my coin, I would slowly, carefully inch open the corresponding door and take a discreet peek inside. If I was lucky enough to have chosen the women's first, I'd duck inside. If not, I'd quickly shut the door and slip into the other one.

"It's a good plan," I told myself. "Foolproof."

A few seconds later I was joined in the corridor by an English fellow with a Caesar haircut and black bomber jacket lined in orange nylon so ubiquitous during the nineties. I smirked to myself as I watched him duck his head back and forth between the doors, struggling, as I had, to work out which was which.

"Any idea which is the gents?" he asked.

"Which is more like a man?" I said absently, twirling a stray piece of windblown hair. "Is it the gorilla or the snake?"

He laughed and gave me the sort of leering look favored by grown men who wear Bart Simpson T-shirts. "Pretty obvious, innit?"

"No," I said coldly.

He stopped laughing and scrunched up his brow, studying the murals in earnest. "The gorilla is the ladies'," he said finally. "There's that—wotsit?—that saying about the mother gorilla?"

"Oh! Oh! I know!" I said sarcastically. "What's that thing about the mother—wotsit?—snake? There's nothing about a mother gorilla. It's a mother bear. That's what you're thinking of."

"A bear is kind of like a gorilla," the man said in a meek voice.

"Both mammals?" I said, sighing.

"And both furry," the man added.

He paused for a minute. "And they both have legs."

"Thanks," I said. "That helps."

THIS IS A cautionary tale. It's a story about symbols and what they mean. It's about the perils of trying to redefine what things mean. It's about communication and how mixed up it can become when one or more parties fails—or refuses—to speak the lingua franca. It's a tale of desperation and hope. A tale, perhaps, of two cities. A snake's tale—or tail. Ha-ha.

"Where does the snake end and the tail begin?" Amy asked.

"Is a snake an animal with a really long neck and a short body or a short neck and a really long body?" Amy asked.

"You're getting way off track," I said, wagging my finger. "You're supposed to be telling me which bathroom you would have chosen if you had nothing to go on but your wits."

"Who cares?" she said. "Obviously someone was just trying to be funny."

"Seriously," I said. "When was the last time you saw someone trying to be funny in France? They were trying to be philosophical. And I didn't get it. Don't you see how much this bugs me? It's like being one of those clueless characters interviewed by Borat. I don't like feeling like an idiot. I like things to make sense."

"No," Amy said, "what you like is to spend 10 years going in circles over the same question that can never be answered. It's only a mural. Don't you have anything more important to think about?"

"Two murals," I said. "And no, not really."

WHAT DOES IT mean to communicate? If no one understands you, are you communicating? If you're standing in a roomful of Farsi speakers screaming in English and no one understands you, you are not communicating. So what are you doing? The short answer: making a fool of yourself.

As surprising as it may seem, though, there are a number of people in the world who, while claiming a desire to put certain ideas across, have almost no concern at all for their listeners. These are the people who, as writers, "write for themselves," the people who claim that they "don't care what other people think." News flash: if you're attempting to communicate a thought or idea, your audience does in fact matter.

In other words, if you want to have two separate ladies and gents bathrooms in the privacy of your own home and you wish, for some reason, to distinguish these by use of gorilla and snake murals, go for it. But if you're operating in a public place, maybe it's best to use symbols that actually mean something to people.

"Calm down," Amy said. "You're hyperventilating."

RECENTLY I WAS talking with a woman I know from church. She told me how another church member called her one afternoon and spent 20 minutes explaining why she shouldn't wear a wedding ring. The gist of the argument? In ancient Babylon prostitutes wore bands of gold around their fingers. Therefore, according to this woman, wearing a wedding ring signifies that you are a prostitute.

Yeah, well, except that it doesn't. If you randomly selected 1,000 people off the street in Britain or America and showed them a hand sporting a gold band, virtually 100 percent of them would indicate that the ring signifies marital status. I'm willing to wager that no one would equate "gold band" with "hooker."

And yet, in Christianity, where there sometimes seems to be an unofficial race to see who can find the most sinister undertones in the most ordinary of objects, this kind of argumentation isn't as rare as you might hope. Christmas is upon us, and I'm sure many of us will be accosted by at least one earnest stranger eager to impress upon us the "pagan" origins of most Christmas traditions. Pagans had feasts. Pagans had trees and wreaths. Pagans exchanged gifts. And if I were the betting kind, I'd wager that pagans drank water and wore clothes and slept at night, too. So what? I hardly know what a pagan is. Surely symbols themselves don't matter. Under every symbol is an idea. The word "love" is a symbol. The idea is eternal; the symbol can vary greatly, depending on which language you speak.

Symbols mean only what society agrees they mean. A red ribbon folded into a tight loop with two splayed ends? That symbolizes support for the fight against HIV/AIDS. Now, it's entirely possible—probable, even, given that there's nothing new under the sun—that ancient Babylonians or even pagans used a similar symbol to indicate human sacrifice. But neither a red piece of ribbon nor a band of polished gold have any inherent moral character or meaning beyond what we assign to them.

There's no point in trying to insist on variant meanings, unless you happen to be the charismatic genius who got everyone saying "bad" when they mean "good." In that case, aren't you the clever magpie.

I KNOW MANY people who do not wear wedding rings for a variety of reasons, and I don't particularly wish to pick on them. People do what they do. They have their reasons. No one needs to explain their actions to me. In fact, sometimes—when the "ancient Babylon" school of thought is invoked—I would rather they didn't.

But what makes me laugh—and maybe even cry a little sometimes—is the delusional insistence by some who believe that they are actually communicating a certain idea to the wider world by not wearing a wedding ring. Or by not having fun on Sabbath—or a zillion other little practices that are very significant to us but that communicate very different ideas to people who are technically not us.

The wedding ring example is an easy one. One of the more common arguments against wedding rings—more common, fortunately, than the "ancient Babylonian prostitute" line—is the idea that wedding rings are "adornment" and that wearing one constitutes an attempt to "draw attention to oneself."

The problem with this is that you have only to spend an afternoon or so walking around actually wearing a wedding ring to observe how little attention it draws. If this is your way of gaining attention, I'm thinking you'd be better served by getting a facial tattoo. Or a Porsche.

A wedding ring, in our present-day culture, signifies one thing: that the wearer is married. If a stranger sees you wearing one, this is likely the only thing about you they will conclude. If they see you without one, likely the only thing they will conclude is that you are single. Not that you are humble. Or thrifty. Or spiritual. Or a Christian. Single.

We Christians—and of course here I'm referring mostly to Adventist Christians—always speak in such hopeful terms of the possibility that people might "notice" that we are "different." But sometimes I think we have a weird way of picking out only certain things to be "different" about. Right off, it isn't entirely clear to me why, out of all the things we could use to distinguish ourselves, we'd particularly want to be confusing over our marital status. And nothing draws attention more than a big hat covered with feathers and silk roses and plastic birds, but you see plenty of those in church. Doncha?

Furthermore, isn't the wish to be noticed—singled out, even—as "different" a desire to draw attention to yourself? So do we want attention or not? Because if you want to deflect attention, the best and easiest way is simply to go with the flow. Do as the Romans do. Just don't—no matter what, do as, you know, the Babylonians do. Or, technically, did.

IN ANOTHER CITY, in another time, in a generic U.S. shopping mall, I was flipping through a rack of sweaters when a young man appeared almost as if from nowhere and handed me a small card. The card said, "Hello. I am a deaf-mute. I am selling seashell key rings to raise money to help deaf-mute people like myself. They cost one dollar. Would you like to buy one?" I gave him the dollar.

If that young man had used the skulky Christian method of "communication," he would have stood around hoping that I would somehow "notice" his disability and ask if there was maybe anything I could do for him. Then when that didn't work, he would have approached me and signed his request in American Sign Language, which I would not have understood. He would have gone away disappointed, and I would have gone away perplexed. That's a lose-lose interaction.

It's important to spend some time thinking about what your values are—not what they look like, but what they are. Like the question of being "different," or "peculiar." In what way exactly? This is a phrase that gets thrown around a lot, but I'm not sure what it means. If I'm to communicate anything about my faith, I have to be clear on what about my faith makes me different and why that's good or important. We don't have to be different from other people in every way. In fact, we can't. It is better to find what we have in common with others, to find our humanity. It is better to bridge chasms than to create them where none really exist. It is better to speak a language that our listeners understand. If we can't do that, well, why not?

"I GIVE UP," Amy said. "Which was the ladies' bathroom—the gorilla or snake?"

I shrugged. "Can't remember."

"You can't remember? What do you mean, you can't remember?"

"Words are symbols," I said. "This particular string of words—I can't remember—symbolizes the fact that I have a brain disorder."

"Do you ever," Amy said.

LIFE WITH DOE

FOR A LITTLE while, when I was a teen, my best friend was a girl who insisted I call her Doe. In return, she called me Bo.

"Best friends should have cute funny rhyming nicknames," she said.

"OK," I shrugged. My mother always said that I was "easily led." This is true. I am not a person of firm convictions regarding the majority of things. Rhyming nicknames sound kind of pointless to me, but hey, whatever. If I had a bumper sticker, it would say, "Hey. Whatever."

For a while our friendship consisted mostly of sitting in our teacher's closet during study hall, under the guise of preparing a health project and needing a place to "think"—and chatting. Our conversations revolved around the eternal question of whom Doe should date. There were two candidates. Bachelor Number One, Doug, was 23 years old and worked at a pet store. He looked like Tommy Lee of the rock band Mötley Crüe. Bachelor Number Two was called Ray. He looked like Billy Ray Cyrus and wore George Michael-style sunglasses. He was also old—maybe 24. He had one of those flashy red motorcycles that you ride hunched over, hugging the bike. He took corners at more than 100 miles an hour.

If you have not figured this out by yourselves through the information I've provided, let me just say that both Doug and Ray were total creeps. If you have not figured this out from the information I've provided, you, sir, are no Hercule Poirot. You might, however, be a 15-year-old girl. Don't worry—you'll grow out of it.

"Which one should I go out with?" Doe would ask, every day, several times a day. "Doug or Ray?"

"Doug," I'd say, because it starts with a D, and I like alphabetical order and order in general.

"But I love Ray," she'd whine.

"Then go out with Ray."

"But I love Doug."

This went on for probably years.

SOMETIMES I WAS unguarded in my disdain for Doug and Ray, and Doe would let loose on me. "You think you're too good for someone like Doug?" she'd scream.

"Doug's a drug dealer," I'd say.

"And what are you?" she'd ask. "What are you that's so great?"

Well, sometimes it's not so much what you are, but what you're not. I, for one, greatly value certain nots in my friends and neighbors. Not a drug dealer. Not a serial killer. Not a snooker enthusiast. Sometimes a negative really is a positive.

There are numerous books these days on the subject of "toxic friends." Mostly they are characterized as "one-uppers" or "perpetual cancelers." They are accused of dire crimes such as "talking about themselves" and "delivering subtle jabs."

In the case of Doe, we're in fact talking about a "friend" who once tried to kick me—with her feet, this is not a metaphor—out of her car in the middle of the night onto a lonely country road flanked by deep ditches. A friend who tried to punch me in the face more times than I can remember. I always ducked.

You see, there were only three girls in my grade at school, and I was one of them. Doe was the other one, and then there was the serious, studious, musical, talented, and smart girl. She and I are friends today, but back then I didn't want to hang out with the smart academic girl. Doe was blond and popular and, because she'd failed the seventh grade, a whole year older than the rest of us. She got her driver's license earlier. And her mother let her do whatever she wanted.

If you figure Doe was Al Capone, I was the guy in the white suit who carries Al Capone's briefcase and walks three paces behind.

"Ah," my present-day friend Tammy said. "You were the sidekick."

Ever seen *The Lone Ranger*? Probably not. It's an old TV show about a masked man in a tight jumpsuit who rode a horse and fought crime in the Old West. His sidekick was an Indian named Tonto. You always really felt like Tonto should have had his own TV show.

"Get your own gig, Tonto!" you wanted to shout out of sheer frustration as you watched him follow the Lone Ranger, hanging on his every word.

Important life lesson: never be Tonto. Your life may be mundane or tragic or pointless, but it should be yours. It should reflect your values, your interests.

"What if my values and interests revolve around snooker?" you ask.

In that case, I take it all back: you should live someone else's life. Somebody really cool, like Bono.

AL CAPONE NEVER pulled the trigger. The guy in the white suit—he pulled the trigger. Not because he especially wanted to. Because he was told to. Because that's what sidekicks do: they do as they're told.

Once we were in a changing room trying on clothes. All of a sudden Doe opened my purse and slipped a red-striped bikini inside.

"Hey!" I said.

She stood up in one fluid motion and brought her face in close to mine. "Shut up," she said.

"I don't want to take that," I stammered.

"Shut up," she said again in a low, strangled voice. "Make a fuss, and you'll get us both busted. Now you walk out of here like everything is fine. You walk out of here, and you don't flinch. Do it."

What she said was not strictly true. If we'd been caught, there would have been no "we." I would have gotten in trouble. I was carrying the bag, after all. It was my bag.

But back then it was so much easier simply to follow the orders of another. It seemed almost wrong to attempt moral superiority. My friend knew this, and she mocked my hesitance: "What? You think you're too good to shoplift a bikini? You think you're better than me? Who do you think you *are*, anyway?"

I walked out the glass doors of the shopping mall clutching my purse. My heart was pounding, and I felt dizzy with fear. But I wore a placid, innocent expression, as if I hadn't a care.

When we got to the car, Doe held out her hand without a word, and I unzipped my purse and slapped the tiny wad of fabric into her outstretched palm. She wore the swimsuit all summer, and no one was ever the wiser.

ONCE DOE AND I were out driving around in her car at 2:00 a.m. on a Sunday morning. She decided to mosey on over to her boyfriend-from-seventh-grade's house and knock on his window. I don't know what she said to him, but he called the police. Two of them came, clicking their heels in unison, like toy soldiers. When Doe screamed and threw bark at them, they determined she was unfit to drive.

I had just received my license a week earlier. One of the cops approached me and narrowed his eyes. He shone a thin light in my face.

"Tilt your head back and touch your fingers to your nose," he said.

"Recite the alphabet backward," he said.

"Quick: what's seven times nine?" he asked. "Four times six?"

He gave his partner a quick nod. "She's OK."

He focused his attention back on me. "We're letting you go," he said. "But you are driving, do you understand? She is not to get behind that wheel." He gestured at Doe, who was lying in the grass, crying and kicking her legs.

Doe's car was a manual. I did not know how to drive a manual. I still struggled to escape a gas pump without taking the door off. I wanted to ask the policemen to take us home. I wanted to fall at their feet and beg their mercy, to confess that if I drove the car, we'd probably kill ourselves and anyone else unlucky enough to be on the same route.

If I'd done that, we would both have gotten in trouble. Doe's parents would have probably taken her car away. I'd have been grounded for at least five years. But that would be the least of my problems, I mused. Doe would likely bludgeon me to death with a brick in my sleep if I got her busted. I weighed my options and found honesty wanting.

"No problemo," I told the cop with a confident swagger manufactured to build his trust in me. "I'm all over it."

He stared me down with bright-blue eyes. "Drive real slow," he said. "Believe it or not, we don't get any big kick scraping you kids off the pavement."

I DIDN'T EXACTLY crash Doe's car, but I did fail to depress the brake along with the clutch while shifting gears and taking a sharp corner simultaneously. We hit the grass and concrete median and went airborne for a second or two. We came down with a thud, facing perpendicular to the road. There was no one around to see. If there's no one watching and you have an accident, does it count? 'Fraid so. The bottom of the car was all scraped up, and it ran a little rough the rest of the way home. Strangely, this was perhaps the only time she didn't scream at me.

After that, our friendship had just one last dramatic scene before I went away to college and we gradually lost touch. She came to my house to borrow a couple of dresses. I was not home. I was at the house behind my parents' house, taking instructions from the mother of a child I was going to be babysitting for the day.

Just as the mother was explaining how to use the microwave, we heard a torrent of foul language coming from the other side of the fence. It was summer and hot. All the windows were open. The stream of bad words was occasionally punctuated by my name. Not Bo. My real name. Becky.

Turns out Doe couldn't find the dresses she wanted to borrow and assumed that I'd hidden them on purpose just to annoy her. She stood on my deck and screamed and shouted and threw empty planters at the fence.

"So," I said to the mother, trying to act nonplussed. "Where do you keep the baby wipes?"

"Honey," my neighbor said gently, patting my shoulder. "You need to get some new friends."

THERE'S A LOT going on in the world. Enormous suffering. Tons of people who need our help and support. Our friendship, even. I'm not advocating a life of selfishness. I'm not really saying you should do only what you please all day every day. Of course we live for others. But not just any Joe off the street has a right to a claim on you.

I'm always a little stunned at people who act as though a religious faith based—at least in part—on trying to be a morally decent person is "cheap" or "easy." In my experience, it's pretty hard to be a good person, difficult to make good choices consistently. It gets even harder when you surround yourself with people who couldn't make a good decision if it came with a free toaster.

Take, for example, an incident I had a few years ago when I was in London. A crackhead with bright eyes and crusty white lips approached me outside Leicester Square Station. It was early morning, and there were few people about.

"I want to talk to you in the alley," he said. "Just come over here for a minute. Please."

At first I hedged, trying to be polite, hoping he would go away. It became increasingly obvious, however, that I was going to have to do one of two things: (1) follow the crackhead into the alley or (2) say no. Neither of these options was particularly attractive, especially since I find confrontation so unpleasant. It may be hard to believe, but for a second or two I actually considered just going into the alley in order to avoid the big blowout that was sure to come.

But then I thought, *You know what? I don't* want *to go into the alley. I want to stand right here.*

And this, sometimes, is what your whole life comes down to—what someone else wants and what you want. You've probably been taught, since you were old enough to toddle—and especially if you're a girl—that other people's wants are more important than yours. Rubbish. If you don't want to do something, don't do it. Dig your heels in until the dirt is spilling into the backs of your shoes. It gets easier.

Even now, I feel almost dirty suggesting that I am, in fact, too good to put up with certain kinds of treatment from certain people and that I should stay away from them. God, we are told, loves Idi Amin just as much as he loves Mother Teresa. Therefore we should love everyone too.

This reminds me of a sort of geometry I learned about in high school—a geometry that exists in outer space, where the sum of a triangle's angles come to either more or less than 180 degrees. It's an interesting idea, and I've no doubt it's true, but here on earth the sum of a triangle's angles is 180 degrees. And here on earth, if I have to pick a friend, I'm not so sure there's any compelling reason for it to be Idi Amin.

Unless wearing a "pretty cool" military dictator uniform counts as a "compelling" reason.

And yes, I know he's dead.

"I'M NOT GOING into the alley," I said finally in a loud voice. "I'd like to stand right here, if you don't mind." The crackhead did mind. He went ballistic. Screaming. Calling me names. Eyes bugging out. Spit dripping down his chin. The usual.

This is one of the easiest ways to spot nonstarters, as far as friendship is concerned. They will always act as though you owe them something even if you don't know them. As soon as you fail to do what these people want, they will turn on you with violence—verbal or physical. Those who behave this way are not potential friends and are possibly dangerous.

Remember that people are God's creatures, and they are infinitely important. And you are one of them. You are not outside the concept of "people." If people are precious, you too are precious. And some people, while no doubt valuable to God, are rotten individuals who do bad things and do not have your welfare at heart. For whatever reason, they choose the dark side. You can't necessarily fix them. And—particularly if you are a teenager or a young person—it ain't your responsibility.

Maybe some people you can love from a distance. Maybe sometimes all you can do is save yourself. "What if everyone thought that way?" you ask. "The world would be a terrible, awful place."

No, it wouldn't. It would be a place where vicious people have to play nice before they can expect to have any friends. Works for me.

Change of plans, I thought. *I'm not going to stand here after all. I'm going to . . . run!*

I ran to Piccadilly Circus Station and was rescued by a one-legged security guard in an orange vest. It was Heather Mills-McCartney. Kidding. It was actually just some lovely old bloke with a red nose.

"That's aw-wight, luv," he said as he held my arm and limped me down the escalator to my train.

But the point is, as I was fleeing and the man was lurching along behind me shouting that he was going to cut my throat, etc., he also threw out one other phrase: "You think you're too good for me?"

And my lips curled back over my teeth in a big smile, and I picked up the pace a little. "Yes," I breathed.

WEAR IT WELL

ELECTIVES, COLLEGE CLASSES that have nothing to do with either your major or minor areas of study, help to give you a broad base of "knowledge." They also help when you transfer temporarily, as I did, to a very small overseas college in your third year and find that most of the relevant courses available are ones you've already done and you need something to fill in your timetable so you won't be deported—which, in spite of how fun it sounds, doesn't necessarily involve boats or any sort of marine travel.

And electives help when you plan, as I did, to spend most of your time filthy, carrying a backpack, and sleeping in train compartments and on coaches (seeing the world for 100 quid) and you don't want to expend much energy reading Thucydides. And when you know your blood sugar will be so low you won't have the mental focus necessary to memorize names, dates, or battles.

This is how I—a humanities person, sometimes known as "artsy"—found myself, much to my amusement, in the world of "business"—a world that wears a uniform and speaks a language as confusing as Pig Latin. You think outside the box. You consider the bottom line. You get on the same page as others. You take the 50,000-foot view of a situation. You remember that there's no "I" in "team." You're proactive rather than reactive. Winners Train; Losers Complain. "What are you talking about?" you want to scream. And everyone wonders why so many people these days sniff glue or take antidepressants.

My elective was Consumer Behavior, which sounds like a dawdle, doesn't it? You think to yourself, *Hey, I'm a consumer. I guess I know a thing or two about consumer behavior.* That's what I thought. But as it turned out, this class wasn't so much about consumer behavior as it was about the various obsessions of the lecturer. I list them in order of importance determined by the number of times they came up in class discussions: (1) Americans are stupid;

(2) fancy fonts are essential in business documents; (3) you'll never succeed unless you adopt the "business uniform."

Number one was so frustrating and annoying to me that I'd often leave the classroom scarcely able to breathe. The first day, I raised my hand after a particularly obnoxious comment. "Excuse me," I said. "I don't really know what this 'business' thing is you're talking about, but I have a sneaky hunch that Americans are pretty good at it."

Now fonts. My first report was criticized in front of the entire class for "lack of fonts." According to my lecturer, when preparing a business document you use "a lot" of different fonts. "Learn to use fancy fonts," she said, waving a sample report in my face. The report, on Madame Tussauds, contained maybe 14 different fonts of various sizes and colors and could probably have caused fits of epilepsy in susceptible individuals. It is unfortunate that there were no such individuals present for me to test my theory on, but I stand by it nonetheless.

"Those ones that look like wieners and stuff?" I asked.

"Exactly," she said.

My instructor was also very keen on what she called "the business uniform." For women, this meant a navy-blue skirt suit, flesh-colored stockings, heels, hair scraped back from the face with a headband, and no makeup.

"You want, as much as possible," she said, "to resemble a male."

At the end of the term we each had to present a "case study" on a consumer-behavior-related topic to the rest of the class. We would not be graded purely on the quality of content, but also on "presentation" (read "lots of fancy wiener-shaped fonts" and the "business uniform").

Of course, I had nothing to wear. I was far from home on a study holiday. I had jeans with holes. Tank tops. Doc Martens. Birkenstocks. A bandanna to wear pirate-style over my unwashed hair. A mangy coat made to look like it was cut from a Navajo Indian blanket. And I had no money with which to purchase a "business uniform." Even a cheap one would have cost the same as a coach ride to Dublin.

"I need a business uniform," I moaned to my best friend one afternoon when we were sunbathing on the grass with lemon juice caked in our hair to make it blond.

"Whazzat?" she asked through half-closed, sleepy eyes.

"Blue skirt suit. Old-lady tights. Heels."

"Yuck," she said. "I wouldn't wear that if you paid me."

"Hey," I said. "There's no 'I' in 'team.'"

On the day of the presentation, I borrowed a business uniform from my roommate, who was proportioned differently than me. In other words, the suit was too big and made me look like a small child dressed in her mother's clothes. I squeezed into a pair of thick, flesh-colored tights, scrubbed my face clean, and scraped my hair back with a thick plaid band.

On the way to the lecture hall I passed a number of people, including the man who is now my husband, and they all laughed at my ridiculous appearance. "You look like an idiot" were, I believe, my future husband's exact words, and it was the insight and accuracy of those words that made me love him. "You think?" I snarled as I stomped up the stairs to the lecture hall with my folder of overhead slides and notes.

I didn't feel very confident, because I looked stupid, and moreover, I didn't look like me. I probably often look stupid, but as long as it's the kind of stupidity I'm comfortable with, my confidence remains intact.

Anyway, I did the best I could—which wasn't very good. The headband—pressing behind my ears—made my head ache so badly I struggled to see my notes. I felt dizzy. My tights itched. My skirt kept sliding low on my hips, and I feared it would fall off.

After my presentation finished, there was a moment of silence while the instructor struggled to compose something positive to say. She finally complimented my spoken English—in front of a class of nonnative speakers. She was also a nonnative speaker. Her compliment was more of a nod to chance than a reflection of genuine achievement. It was like being congratulated for wearing size eight shoes.

"Thanks," I said. "You ought to see me roll my tongue."

I slumped into my chair in defeat and began to mentally prepare myself for the inevitable mediocre B grade.

And I have to tell you, all these years later, I still blame my underwhelming performance on the business uniform.

"You don't think it might have something to do with how you don't even know what business is?" someone ventured recently.

No. I don't believe I know what anything is. Not really. Never have. But I got lots of A grades anyway.

"That doesn't speak very well for the educational system," you say.

Sigh.

THERE ARE A couple of truths about personal appearance: (1) it is very important; (2) it isn't important at all.

"But those are opposing ideas!" you say. "You can't believe both of those propositions simultaneously!"

Oh, no? Watch me.

Let's start with the idea that how you look is important.

Duh.

As I've just demonstrated by way of my helpful consumer behavior anecdote, feeling uncomfortable about your appearance can lead to a poor performance.

Nowadays I'm much better at performing well even when I look horrible (and after all, I've had two kids, so it's not like I've had much of a choice), but I still notice what a difference I feel if I'm able to present myself the way I want to. If I'm in an outfit that makes me look thin. If my hair is good. If I look the way I think I ought to look.

It is, I think, a basic human right to determine how you will present yourself to the world. This is why institutions that rely on stomping out any sense of the individual like uniforms. A uniform shreds a little of your confidence. It erodes your feeling of uniqueness—that just like a snowflake, there is no one else quite like you. And when you lose your sense of individuality, you're easier to control. This is why I don't like uniforms. Not at school or work or in prison. Not the Mao suit.

But the business uniform is, I'll admit, a little different. For one thing, it isn't issued. You can pick a variation of it for yourself. If I'd had the money or the will, I could have bought myself a business uniform that fit properly and was flattering, and I might have done a little better with my presentation.

And no matter how stupid I think the business uniform is, there is no doubt that other people judge you on presentation, and it affects everything in your life. Your job. How you get treated in Debenhams, at the doctor's office. Maybe even at church.

If I'm meeting with clients or doing any kind of work that involves being around people, I don't wear pajamas. I dress up and make sure I look capable and respectable. This is just good common sense.

In Hemel Hempstead, where I lived for a number of years, there was a man with tattoos and small metal rings covering his entire face. Once I was exiting Sainsbury's just as he was entering, and I almost bumped into him.

When I saw his face, I actually gasped, involuntarily, out loud. Now, this man might be a great guy. He might be really smart and talented and good with pets and small children. But probably no one ever gives him a chance to prove any of those qualities. I doubt if he has a job.

So how you look is important: both in terms of how you see yourself and how others see and respond to you. This extends particularly to your choice of clothing and accessories, which is the part of your appearance over which you exercise the most control.

But just because that's true doesn't mean there's any excuse—any excuse at all—for being fashion-obsessed. You know what drives me even more nuts than "there's no 'I' in 'team'"? It's the sections in magazines that list "must-haves" for the season and lecture you on which color is the "new" black. Or worse, the sections that inform you which of your various body parts are now "in." As in "Shoulders are in this season." Huh?

Maybe you can't ever become the kind of person who is so comfortable with who you are that you can be spotty and stinky and wearing too-short, high-waisted jeans and a wrinkly mustard-yellow blouse with a ruffle around the neck and still feel confident and sure that you have value, but that doesn't mean you have to be a fashion victim.

It doesn't mean you should feel like a loser because you don't have anything brown when brown's the new black or that the "must-have" section of a magazine deserves anything more than a sneer and a quick turn of the page.

Get in the habit of muttering, "Don't you tell me what I *must* have. The only thing I must have is the ability to hold my head up, and they don't sell that at Harvey Nicks."

Learn to, you know, think outside the box. What box? You know, *the box.*

TIME ON YOUR HANDS

WHEN A FRIEND popped by my house to deliver some homemade mango ice cream, she was stunned to discover I'd just painted my kitchen. With my own two hands—and occasionally, my right foot. My elbow got a look in too.

"Wow," she said. "You are so bizarre. I would never just get up one day and think, *Hey, I'm going to paint the kitchen.*"

"Mmm," I said, mouth full of ice cream.

"You must have *a lot* of time on your hands."

How's that for a kick in the teeth? If it weren't for the ice cream—and the fact that I love my friend dearly—I might have been upset. And when I say "upset," I mean I might have thrown something (a trivet?) through my kitchen window.

Take a moment and think back to how many times you've heard "you/he/she must have a lot of time on your/his/her hands"—or a variation—over the past few weeks. Have you ever heard it said in an admiring tone? Is it ever a compliment? If someone were to accuse you of having "a lot of time on your hands," how would you feel?

I'll bet you'd feel defensive. Irritated. Perhaps diminished in some way. You might stew about it for days. I can almost guarantee you wouldn't flash a relaxed smile and say, "Why, thank you. Yes, I do have an abundance of time. Aren't I the lucky sloth?"

The cult of busyness rules us all. It determines how we judge ourselves and others. I don't mean to say there's anything wrong with activity or the prospect of a day filled with accomplishments, no matter how small. There are things to be done, and we—all of us—have to do them. This is a fact.

But here's another fact: being busy does not make you important. Having a to-do list the length of a small playing field is not synonymous with mattering. So why do we think it is?

When people ask us how we are and we say "Swamped" or "Shattered" or "Rushed off my feet," what are we really saying?

It is no small wonder that stay-at-home mothers and retired people are some of the worst offenders when it comes to being "busy." The only possible justification for taking "leisure" time is an astonishingly high salary. When you're not earning, there's even more pressure to carve your existence into the nearest rock, to make sure everyone knows that you matter. And why do you matter? Because every minute of your day is accounted for. You are accomplishing things. As long as you never stand still, you won't dissolve into oblivion.

But funny enough, even high earners get caught up in busyness. Bill Gates, the richest man in the world, when asked in an interview whether he was religious, answered no. He went on to say, "Just in terms of allocation of time resources, religion is not very efficient. There's a lot more I could be doing on a Sunday morning."

I know just what he means. I grew up in a home and community in which Sabbath observance was important, but even so, I often feel frustrated with having to slow down that one day a week. *What's the point of this?* I wonder. I struggle to avoid spending my "day of rest" mentally ticking off all the things I need to do just as soon as it's over. After all, if I slow down I might dissolve. No one will love or respect me. I won't matter.

When you endlessly rant about how "swamped" you are, you're really rather pathetically seeking approval and status from others. "I'm important," you plead in a whiny voice. "People depend on me. If I were run over by a bus, this whole place would fall to pieces."

It's important to face the truth. Life will go on without you and your one-man/one-woman whirlwind. Eventually your time—that time you so liberally fill with errands and "important" duties—will run down. You won't have "too much time on your hands." It will all be over, and you will be remembered for a while, by those who loved you, but eventually, no matter how many things you accomplished—unless you did something truly extraordinary or bizarre—no one will care how busy you were.

Elizabeth I died in 1603. Her last words were "All my possessions for a moment of time."

Time isn't something to burn up or kill. You can never have "too much." The problem for all of us is that we'll never have enough. So why apologize or feel guilty for stopping to unwind, to figure out what it all means, maybe to ask a question or two? Maybe even to paint your kitchen with your own two hands if that's what rings your bell.

For quite a while now I have had a goal. This goal is to stop talking about how busy I am. I haven't quite managed it yet. The cult of busyness is far too seductive, and even when I know—with as much certainty as I've ever known anything—that being busy doesn't matter, I still find myself sucked into believing that I'll be something more than what I am if I can only move fast enough.

I'm ashamed to admit it, but I couldn't resist defending myself to my friend about painting the kitchen.

"Actually I'm swamped," I said, licking the back of my ice-cream-covered spoon. "Now I'm really behind. Tons of projects to do. I'm going to be up late every night this week."

I see myself uttering these ridiculous words, and I don't know whether to laugh or be disgusted.

If one day I can bring myself to say, "I'll take all the free time I can get and soak it up and love it; I am not defined by my errands," then maybe I'll be somewhere close to becoming the person I want to be.

Until then, I guess I'll just be busy. Swamped. Run off my feet.

HAIR YOU ARE

I WAS IN the basement pounding out "Silver Bells" on the piano in preparation for the much-dreaded annual Christmas recital when my father came home from work with an important announcement.

"We're moving," he said.

I didn't even ask where to or require any details. It could have been Tierra del Fuego for all I cared. My parents watched anxiously for my reaction, clearly worried about taking me away from my school and friends.

Fact One: I had no friends.

Fact Two: I was the most pathetic, worthless, creepiest little person in the entire United States, including West Virginia—or so I believed.

Fact Three: I desperately wanted a chance to start over, to "reinvent" myself, as Madonna Ciccone might put it.

Fact Four: I had only just celebrated my eleventh birthday.

Children tend to be awkward at this time of life, and I was more awkward than most. I had the unfortunate tendency to turn bright red when embarrassed—and I was almost daily humiliated in one way or another. "I hate Becky," I remember a classmate saying. "She's always turning red."

Still, up until fifth grade, I'd survived socially. In first and second grade I had a best friend, and we played together every day. In third grade, though, I made a fatal mistake. A new girl joined our class, and I dumped my old best friend for her. The summer before fifth grade started, this new friend moved to Missouri—and I was left with no one. During recess I sat alone in the breezeway while my former best friend and a few other girls made a point of ignoring me. Worst of all, I knew I deserved it.

So when my father came home with the news that we were moving more than 100 miles south and that I would attend a new school, I was ecstatic at the idea of escape. I went to my room and switched off the lights and tucked my head behind my curtain to look out at the winter sky. I gazed at the center star in Orion's sword—the star I'd been taught was the gateway to heaven.

"Dear God," I whispered. "Please, please, if You care about me at all, please don't let me be a creep or a loser. This time, I just want to be popular."

NOT HAVING READ any teen or women's magazines, I didn't realize that when you embark on a "new beginning" the first thing you need is a whole new image.

A "look," as the fashionites like to call it. Foolishly I assumed that the mere difference in setting would increase my chances of a power position in the new school hierarchy. I had little concept of style, clothing, hairstyles, or fashion in general, and I wore whatever my mother bought me. My hair was long and poker-straight, with a severe fringe across my eyebrows.

I played with dolls. I carried a Strawberry Shortcake lunch box. Worst of all, as it turns out, I wore a red Eskimo-style coat with a faux fur-fringed hood. I stood in front of the entire class wearing it and holding my lunch box while the principal introduced me. This was 1983, and the latest fashion in outerwear was pastel-colored ski jackets with turnup collars. The class stared at me. Someone snorted. Someone else threw a spitball when the teacher's back was turned, and it got caught in the faux fur of my hood.

"Nice coat," one of the older kids sneered as she brushed by me in the hallway on my way outside for recess.

Within the first week I learned that not only was my coat "uncool," but so was almost all my other stuff. Stuff was important in this school. Just like ketchup is important at McDonald's.

Nobody carried a lunch box; they brought disposable brown paper sacks. They wore oversized neon yellow, green, and pink sweatshirts with leggings and matching bandannas rolled up and tied around their hair, Alice-band style, with a funky knot on the top. Everyone had a plastic, pastel-colored comb sticking out of his or her back pocket.

Most important, they wore their hair in perfect eighties mullets: layered, feathered, and waved. They spent every break in the bathroom, obsessively grooming their hair and often sharing combs. This, by the way, is how I contracted head lice. But that, perhaps, is another story, for another late-night session of humiliation and self-pity.

I studied the cool kids the way an anthropologist might observe the movements of a particularly perplexing tribe—writing everything down in

163

detail in cramped print and hoping to make sense of it all back at the office.

My mom took me shopping for the neon clothes, a new ski jacket, and a purple plastic unbreakable comb. All that was left, to make my transformation complete, was a whole new hairstyle. Farrah Fawcett-esque.

My first appointment, at a local salon cleverly called Hair We Are, had to be canceled when my grandfather died. My mom called me at school, sobbing, to explain why she couldn't pick me up for my appointment. I started crying too, and my grief was genuine, but it was more about my hair than it was about my grandfather.

Wow, I think to myself as I write those words. *You were—and are—such an unbelievable jerk. How can you bear to have the world—well, the world who reads this stuff, anyway—know the truth about you?*

Oh, I don't know. Maybe I think the truth about me is obvious anyway. Maybe I believe the truth about me is the truth about everyone. Maybe I just want to tell you—whoever you are—simply this: It's OK. And if it's not, it will be.

"What are you talking about? I'm nothing like you! I'm the anti-you," you say.

Hey, fair enough. And, well, uh . . . mazel tov.

THE PART ABOUT all of this—the ski jacket, the comb, my hair—that is so dumb is that I already had several new friends. Three girls in my class had taken a special interest in me from the first day, inviting me to join in their foursquare game at recess, and, in fact, practically fighting over who got to sit next to me on the bus. I liked these girls—all of them—and spent hours giggling with them over private jokes and pictures of Michael Jackson, who at that time was considered "sexy," not that I had even the vaguest notion of what that adjective meant. My mother took one look at a pinup of the King of Pop and sniffed, "Doesn't look to me like he'd have the faintest idea what to do with a woman." And I thought, *Huh?*

Simply having friends wasn't enough for me. I wanted the rubber-stamping that comes when the whole school—bar no one—approves. Admires, even. I don't believe I cared whether they liked me. I just wanted—needed, really—for them to acknowledge my "coolness." For someone to say, "OK, you can stop now. You're done. You've arrived."

"For someone to say 'Hair you are'?" you ask.

You got it in one, buckaroo.

"WHAT HAPPENED WITH your hair?" my 7-year-old son asks eagerly whenever I get to this point in the story. He knows the answer, of course. He loves this story like he loves the stories of my broken bones, grazed hands, and deep oozing head injuries.

Maybe it's because he looks at me and I appear to be a grown-up, the kind who works and drives a car and is eligible to vote, and maybe it helps him to know that once I was broken and bleeding and insignificant and stupid.

Yet I'm still standing, more or less upright, like a full-fledged human being.

Back then things were significantly more dicey. The school bus dropped me off at Hair We Are, and my mother joined me outside. Together we met with the stylist, and I explained how I wanted my hair to look.

It seems important to mention that I've had some less-than-successful hairdressing experiences. Once, in Bracknell, halfway through my cut, the stylist informed me that her dead mentor had sent her a message through mental telepathy informing her that the way I wanted my hair was all wrong for my face. "So we're going to do something a little different," she said, angling the scissors dangerously toward my neck.

Just putting two and two together, I would have to conclude that the stylist at Hair We Are also had a dead mentor—or at least a very demented one.

Fact One: I said "feathered."

Fact Two: I said "Farrah Fawcett."

Fact Three: At no point did I express a secret wish to look like Little Orphan Annie.

Fact Four: I had only just celebrated my eleventh birthday. What kind of perverse individual gives an 11-year-old girl an old-lady perm and then puts her in rollers under a hot-air dryer?

My first clue that the hairstyling experience was quickly headed south came when the stylist, busily removing the plastic perm rods from my toxic, stinking hair, said, "Wow! Your hair *really* takes a perm." Her voice shook a little.

Also, even though she'd slathered my forehead with petroleum jelly, the perm chemicals had actually burned the skin around my hairline—from ear to ear. Red. Itchy. Stinging. Blistering.

I don't know how I held it together when she finally whirled me around to face the mirror. My red hair was kinked tight around my head like a fuzzy helmet.

I didn't even cry. Looking back, that's the part I can't understand. How is it that I didn't cry? I cry about everything. Maybe it was similar to the way people faced with utterly earth-shattering news—a bad diagnosis, an unexpected monstrous bill—grit their teeth and vow to pull through. When you're faced with annihilation—and no, I'm not being overly dramatic, thanks—the only way you can survive is to focus every ounce of energy on, well, survival.

My dad and brother managed to mask their shock when I crept through the door, hoping to sneak past them. They quickly pulled their faces into the appropriate polite smiles. "Looks great!" they lied. Having the hair stuck, clownlike, on my head was not nearly so bad as watching people pretend to like the hair and having to pretend to like it myself.

Somehow I survived the bus ride to school the next morning, with a baying busload of kids all singing "The Sun Will Come Out Tomorrow." All day long people snorted and smirked and pointed and laughed and hung their heads from classroom windows shouting, "Annie! Look at Annie!"

But my three friends were nice about it. Midway through the day, during recess, we were playing a game that involved a lot of running around, and I suddenly realized that I'd been laughing and having fun for perhaps a full 20 minutes without thinking about my hair. This carefree abandon was short-lived. On the way home a girl threw a wad of sticky pink gum in my curly hair. Tugging at the wad stuck to my head, I exited the bus at the bottom of the hill leading to my house.

"Hair we are!" the bus driver chirped. I don't think he was trying to be mean.

Unfortunately, my mother had to cut out a big chunk right in the middle at the back of my head to remove the gum.

OFTEN I THINK our attempts at "new beginnings"—best expressed in things such as New Year's resolutions—go wonky because of our attitude toward ourselves. We see ourselves, much as I did back then, as desperately pathetic beings who need to be fixed in order to have any intrinsic value.

During my 20s and even early 30s, I felt an instant revulsion at any reminder of my adolescent self. Hanging on what used to be my bedroom wall at my parents' house is a large graduation photo of me taken when I was 18 years old. Coming up to the photo shoot, I read a lot of advice on how to look your best in a photo. You put green cream on blemishes to cancel out the red. You put yellow under your eyes to get rid of dark circles. To make your nose appear slimmer, you draw two dark lines down either side with a white line in the middle. Obviously, you are supposed to blend the lines into your skin.

I blended for the photo, but I still can see these brown lines on my nose. For years the sight of this photo drove me nuts. To think that I had once been the kind of person (reject) who would actually draw brown lines on her nose to make it look thinner. Thinner! I'm losing IQ points just thinking about it.

"I hate that person," I once said to my mother in an offhand remark a few years back. "I look at that picture, and I just hate her. Everything about her. She was such an idiot."

My mother, to my surprise, was deeply upset by this revelation. After some consideration, it became obvious why. For my parents, I am this amazing creature, this miracle even—someone they can scarcely believe they had anything to do with creating. I am the person they have thought about and worried about and taken pride in all these years. Even when I had stupid hair and messed-up teeth. Even when I was failing geometry. Even when I ran away from home and daily shouted "I hate you" in their general direction without going so far as to allow them to think that statement was part of anything approaching an actual conversation.

The idea that my kids might one day hate themselves makes me feel sick with dread. Maybe this is what turned it around for me—I don't know.

What I do know is this: When I see old photos of the me I used to be, when I remember stories like the one I've just told, I've started to allow myself to feel something other than revulsion. Call it a kind of wry fondness. Indulgence, even.

I still believe that a healthy sense of self-loathing is a good and necessary thing. The operative word here is "healthy."

"Self-loathing taken once daily with carrots, barley, and wheatgrass?" you ask.

Why not? But when I say "healthy," I mean balanced with humor, understanding, and affection.

For me, the most important "new beginning" is realizing that, for better or worse, I'm in this personality and this body for life. There are pros and cons—sometimes, when I'm feeling obsessive, even lists of pros and cons. But the older I get, the longer the pro list gets and the more faded, crumpled, and forgotten the con list.

Fact One: I kind of like being me.

Fact Two: I even like that I once had a Little Orphan Annie hairstyle.

Fact Three: The head lice was also pretty hilarious—my mom checked my head for two years.

Fact Four: I am created in God's image, and He loves me unconditionally—even more than my parents love me, and even when I mess up.

WHERE TO STAND

A HASTILY ERECTED chain-link fence separated the two camps. On one side was a group of weepers—mostly women—holding candles and kneeling in prayer, their bodies stretched low to the ground with grief.

I noticed them first. Their flickering candles were visible from the road. *How pathetic,* I thought as I trudged along the icy path leading up to the prison, slivers of glittering frost crunching beneath my weight. This assessment has not softened during the intervening years. I disapprove of public wailing for people one does not personally know—even when the individual in question is Mother Teresa. I more or less simply want to vomit when the object of such abject grief is a pedophile and child murderer.

"But," you say, "how can a person help if they're sad? You feel what you feel." True. But you don't have to feel it in public. You don't—I'm certain—have to feel it with candles.

In Washington State an individual served with a death warrant gets to choose how to die. Behind curtain A you have lethal injection. Swinging behind curtain B is a thick rope and, underneath it, a trapdoor. That night—or to be perfectly correct, early morning—in January 1993 Westley Allan Dodd opted for the rope.

I was 21 years old and going to college only a few miles from the penitentiary—known colloquially as "Concrete Mama." At night they lit the pen so bright I'm certain it could be seen from outer space. This is just surmising, but I'm guessing that people living in houses near the prison don't even have to switch their lights on at night to avoid falling down the stairs on a visit to the bathroom. Think of the household savings on electricity, swallowed instead by the taxpaying public.

As I drew closer to the crowd assembled outside the prison, the weepers began singing "Amazing Grace." On the other side of the fence, where the "death-penalty enthusiasts" stood, I noticed a very tall man—at least six feet five inches—wearing a tattered cowboy hat and a noose arranged art-fully around his neck.

A few months later I moved into an apartment, and my next-door neighbor looked an awful lot like this guy. Creepy cowboy—one eye lower than the other. Without the noose, though, it was difficult to make a positive ID.

TO HAVE THE opportunity for an up-close-and-personal look at the go-ings-on outside a prison on the night of a long-awaited execution seemed like a unique experience for me. Once in a lifetime—like sitting in the au-dience during the Wimbledon final. I suppose I was curious about how ex-tensive the spectacle would be at Concrete Mama. I like to collect experiences, to observe what people say and do, to try to make it all mean something. So I crunched through the frost on a bitter night, wearing san-dals with no socks—I am absentminded to the extreme and often forget suitable footwear—and a long coat buttoned to the chin.

This was not my first visit to the Washington State Penitentiary.

During my first year of college my criminology class took a tour, and we saw lots of those enormous tattooed men—the type often featured in films—who spend their days lifting weights in the "Big Yard." One man stood at the bars of his cell as we passed by and screamed, "This ain't no zoo! Whad-daya looking at? This ain't no zoo!" I very much wanted to say. "Actually, it sort of is," but we were advised not to speak to—or make eye contact with—the prisoners.

And sometimes, when I had nothing else to do or just felt like driving, I'd open my sunroof, blast my music, and head out toward the prison. The wheatfields there are golden and endless. It's an interesting contrast—free-dom and incarceration, wheat bending in the breeze and motionless concrete walls, and men with guns in the towers.

I knew, from having been inside, that the walls are so high you can't tell what's beyond, and I often wondered how many of the prisoners ar-rived at night and how many had no idea they were in the middle of a giant wheatfield.

But I say this more with curiosity than much in the way of pity for the lack of view. I was inside for four hours, and the way a lot of them held their eyes, it was clear they'd just as soon wring my neck as look at me.

ABSURDLY, I WANTED to stop him—the man with the noose—and ask, "Did you tie that yourself? A noose? Where did you learn to do that? Doesn't wearing it make you feel like a morbid freak?" But the atmosphere made my throat close with . . . I don't know what to call it exactly. Try fear. Not a perfect choice of word, but close.

The television does a good job of depicting the signs, placards, frying pans, and firecrackers that accompany this type of event. You see the people pumping their fists in anticipation of one minute past midnight; you hear the great cheer that goes up when the clock strikes. But what the television can't possibly show you is how the air crackles, how the electricity of the crowd's almost rabid anticipation stands your arm hairs on end. The people's eyes glow, and when they laugh and light their string of ladyfingers, what you feel is an icy finger trailing all the way up your spine.

Before that night, I'd read descriptions of atmospheres that have a density, a volume, but I never knew what that meant. Now I know, and I'll never forget the way it enters your nostrils, how it stiffens your back, how you can't relax, how you have to check your soul at the gate. When they give it back, you find it three sizes smaller, and you have to spend weeks tugging it back into shape again.

The chain-link fence dividing the two camps—for and against capital punishment—was also staked out by a row of prison guards, presumably to protect the vigil holders from the hostility of the others. Everyone present seemed to have staked out a territory. They all had a role to play—whether that be weeping, praying, holding candles, wearing nooses, or preparing a long string of firecrackers and readying the match. Then there was me, and my problem was this: I didn't know where to stand.

I couldn't set up camp next to the man with the noose or the people chanting. There was no way I'd wave a candle or sing "Amazing Grace." And that's not to say that even a child murderer can't receive grace—but I've never been a big enough person to wish that with anything approaching sincerity.

I kept wandering between the two camps—each time having to pass through a kind of checkpoint. After a while the guards started looking at me like I was nuts: "Hey, lady! Pick a lane already!" But I couldn't pick a lane. There was nowhere for someone like me to stand. And then I began to wonder what it means to be someone like me—a person who seemingly lacks conviction. Maybe such a person has no business outside a "Concrete

Mama" at midnight in practically her bare feet. I lacked proper footwear. I lacked an objective point of view, the kind you could slap on a bumper sticker.

Would it sound weird if I admitted that sometimes I envy people like the cowboy with the noose? Yeah, I was afraid it might. Allow me to explain: it just seems so comforting somehow, knowing exactly what you think, precisely where you belong. To come to an event, such as this execution, and make a beeline straight for the spot in the gravel with your name on it. To go home afterward, maybe after a stop at the Iceberg for a celebratory chocolate shake, knowing that you carried out the force of your conviction—albeit in a rather juvenile and pointless style—to its logical conclusion.

I can't, however, claim to understand this kind of conviction. Who are these people, I wonder, these brave or foolish souls who so confidently raise their eyes to the heavens and make ironclad pronouncements? "Even God Himself couldn't sink the *Titanic*."

AT ONE MINUTE after midnight the fireworks popped and a great cheer erupted from one side of the fence. On the other side they sang louder. I hopped up and down in place to keep my feet warm and also because the motion made me feel less like I was standing anywhere in particular, even for a moment.

A television reporter approached with a camera crew and asked if I had anything I would like to say for the news. What I wanted to say was "Dude, I don't even know where to stand. How could I possibly begin to know what to say?"

But the truth is, one thing has nothing to do with the other. You don't have to know where you stand on a subject in order to say an awful lot about it anyway. Just open your mouth. Don't worry—something will start spewing out; it always does. Or poise your hands over a keyboard, close your eyes, and think a single thought. Right or wrong, it will lead to another and another and another. Before you know it, you'll have written 2,000 words, but that still doesn't mean that on a frozen night, in almost bare feet, you'd have any idea where to plant those babies.

WHAT DOES THIS tell us about conviction? Not sure. Let me ask you this: What do Martin Luther King, Mahatma Gandhi, Adolf Hitler, and Osama bin Laden have in common? Facial hair? Yes. But something else, too.

They all had conviction. Quite a bit more of it than the average Liam on the street. And it's led to mixed results, right?

As comforting and fuzzy as it might be to have an extremely clear sense of the world and your place in it—a neon sign, so to speak, with your particular path lit in green—it doesn't work that way for all of us. And even for those of you who live that way, it doesn't necessarily work—if by work you mean "create a life of meaning that significantly influences society in a positive way."

I READ SOMEWHERE, and I can't remember where, that we, as Christians, must learn to live "in the tension." And tension you will have if you're the kind of person who cares even a smidge about the way the world is. If you don't care, if you exert all your energy on the plotlines of Coronation Street and never consider anything deeper than what you're having for tea, you won't ever need to know what that means. But most Christians—because we are people who believe that light has come into the world and that it's our duty to help spread that light—will live in the tension. The tension of never knowing for sure if you're doing right. Of often feeling awkward and out of place. Of not knowing just precisely where to stand. Of having awfully cold toes.

"YOU SURE YOU don't want to make a statement?" the television reporter asked. For some reason—just like that—I felt a lot stronger. It was good being me and not knowing or understanding a single thing. I stopped hopping and stood still and felt—maybe not peace, exactly, but acceptance of the fact that my road would be long and winding, with everything always just slightly out of view. I would always be wondering.

"My toes are cold," I said. "I'm going home. Ask someone else. Smart money's on the guy with the noose."

LOSING YOUR DONKEY

ONCE UPON A time there was a family with one young son. They lived out in the middle of nowhere and were so poor they had nothing to eat but beans.

One day the father said, "I hate beans!"

"We do too!" shouted the mother and son.

"I have a plan," the father said. "We'll take our useless donkey to market, sell him, and buy some decent food and some seeds to plant a garden. Son, you will come with me."

Next morning father and son tied a rope around the donkey's neck and headed for the marketplace. Early into the journey they passed a group of people on the road.

"Oh!" one of the people exclaimed, "Look at those two half-wits. If we had a donkey, you think we'd be walking? They should take turns riding the donkey."

The father said, "That is a great idea. I don't know why I didn't think of it myself. I'll let you go first." He hoisted the little boy up onto the donkey.

They carried on for some time and then came upon another group, who said, "Look at that horrible little boy. What is the matter with him? Children today have no respect. The boy should let his poor father ride."

The father frowned. "I suppose it is my turn now," he said. The boy and his father switched places. After a while, they passed a third group of people. "Look at that hideous child abuser! Imagine making a little boy walk! A good father would put the boy in front of him on the donkey. They can both ride."

"I guess there's room for us both," the father said, and he hoisted the boy up.

Yet another group approached to shame them. "Look at those two fatties riding on that donkey. We should call the animal rights authorities. Any decent people—after subjecting an animal to such torment—would carry him the rest of the way."

174

"Oh, dear," the father said sadly. "We had better do as these good people say. We don't want to end up in prison."

They rubbed their rope on a sharp rock until it was separated into two pieces that could be used to tie the donkey's front and hind legs together. They hung him upside down from a pole, which angered the donkey, causing him to roll his eyes, clack his teeth, and swish his tail. Father and son hoisted the pole onto their shoulders and staggered off down the path toward the market.

Coming to a river, they started to wade across, balancing precariously on the slippery rocks, trying not to trip over stumps and tangled debris. In the middle of the river was a large, green, slimy, slippery rock. The pair climbed up onto the rock, but they slipped and lost hold of the donkey. He fell into the shallow but rapidly moving river with a splash and was carried away by a current, down the river and over a waterfall, never to be heard of again.

The poor boy and his father climbed, dejected, out of the river. Water dripped from their hair and clothes.

An old woman, sitting nearby on the bank, cackled and said, "A fool cut in half would have better sense in either end than to try to carry a donkey like that."

Moral? If you try to please everyone, you will end up pleasing no one. You may even lose your donkey. My mother told me this story again and again while I was growing up. "Stop trying to please everyone," she'd say. (But she was always pretty happy if I tried to please her.)

CRITICISM CAN BE difficult to bear. This is particularly true when it comes as a shock, attacking an aspect of your life or work you feel confident in, when you think *How could anyone possibly have a problem with* that? Not too long ago I was surprised to find that an acquaintance thinks I'm a "kook"—surprised not because being thought a kook is anything new, but because the charge was leveled against my parenting style, which, naturally, is beyond reproach.

My eldest son, who is almost 6, is still sometimes frightened of the monsters that he imagines inhabit his closet, lurk under the bed, and climb through his bedroom windows. My solution? I have a bottle of "monster repellent" that I spray in four places before bedtime: windows, closet, door, bed. The monster repellent is lavender room spray. My little boy goes to bed happy, and I don't have to wake up in the night to calm a hysterical child. That's what you call win-win.

But at least one person thinks I should tell my son the truth: monsters don't exist and that's that. I don't want to get into a whole exposition of what I think it means for something to "exist," but let me put it this way: when you awaken in the dark, terrified, that's as real as anything can ever be. As a person with some experience of the dark, I don't live in a world of "should." I want solutions that work. Maybe one could call this approach Machiavellian. I wish one would—it would make me feel awfully important and might even prompt the purchase of a somber, but fetching, black beret.

ON VIRTUALLY ANY medical drama there will come a point at which a whole team of surgeons and nurses are working desperately to save someone's life. "He's bleeding into his thorax!" someone will shout. "Give me 10 cc's of epinephrine!" someone else yells, prompting the audience to wonder, "Huh?"

The lead doctor, the one whose patient is dying and who, at this point, is becoming quite emotional, shouts, "Come on!" and repeatedly pounds the guy's chest with a clenched fist. Within a few minutes all the other doctors and nurses drop their arms to their waists in resigned defeat. They step back from the operating table. Finally someone says, "Dr. Reid, it's your call."

There is a pregnant pause, and the camera zooms in on Dr. Reid, who is sweating and twitching and biting her lip. She struggles with everything that hangs in that moment: to keep fighting or to let go. In one fluid movement Dr. Reid pulls down her surgical mask, looks at the clock, and says, "Time of death, 10:43." She pulls the mask over her head and throws it on the floor, stalking out of the room to scrub her hands at the sink furiously, as if washing away the bitter traces of her failure.

There is a heavy weight on anyone whose role in life involves "making the call." As a parent, I—along with many of you—have to make judgment calls. They are calls that only I can make. Scary, isn't it? You never know, absolutely, that you're doing the right thing. You send up silent prayers, cross your fingers, and hope for the best. I think I'm doing the right thing with the monster repellent, and as it happens, it's my call. Perhaps in 20 years, if my son begins, in any way, to resemble Charles Manson, I may reconsider my position. If he turns out successful, happy, and well adjusted, I'll be chanting, "Na-na, na-na, NAH-NAH!" Perhaps my son's destiny is written into his genes and it doesn't matter what I do; regardless, I have to make a call.

This doesn't, by the way, mean that I don't care what people think or that I'm arrogant enough to dismiss criticism. In fact, the man who doesn't like my monster repellent is a very good father. He has a 100 percent success rate, having raised his impressive children to adulthood. It's not that I think he's wrong; only that I believe there's more than one way to peel an avocado. And as much as I want people to approve of me—and I think we're all inherent people pleasers, even those of us who would pound our shoes on the table Khrushchev-style and violently deny it—I can't change direction every time someone disagrees with my choices. My feelings may be hurt, but I'll go on peeling avocados the best way I know how. Likewise, there's no reason to hate someone for taking a different tack than you might. There's a whole lot of things in this world that, inexplicably and against all odds, just plain work.

A whole army of people can stand on the bank and shout orders and "suggestions," but whether or not your donkey ever makes it to the market—whether you achieve what you set out to do—is up to you. Your call.

If you're going to lose your donkey—and sometimes, despite your best efforts, you will—at least make sure it's on your terms. Rest easy knowing you followed your instincts and that, at the very least, your failure didn't come as a result of holding your finger to the wind.

And give other people a break. Just as you have particular areas in life for which you alone are responsible—and by responsible, I mean you're the one who has to act—so do others. I guess you can go ahead and voice your opinion, but to expect that your particular wisdom be embraced—by the doer—without question is both bizarre and extraordinarily arrogant. Opinions are like ears—everybody's got them. And so what? So what?

Don't be the least bit surprised—let alone offended—when people ignore your advice, moving forward without your permission or blessing, doing what they gotta do. When this happens, nod your head sagely and give a little salute. It takes guts for a person to go their own way, risking the wrath of others. Guts deserve respect. Try to understand the other person's actions if you can. If you can't, just whisper to yourself, "Go safely, my friend. You and your donkey."

COMMUNITY

THE WASHINGTON CONFERENCE camp meeting—the one I attended growing up—takes place on the Auburn Academy campus, just the other side of the Muckleshoot Indian Reservation. The road leading up to the campus is littered with ramshackle houses and rusted cars sunk into weed-infested front yards, sprouting dandelions. They may have cleaned it up a bit since I've been out that way, but for me, this is how it will forever be. This is the way it is in my memory.

The reservation sports a big casino with a main prize—a pink, doublewide trailer with a white door and big brass knocker—rotating on a giant turntable. A flashing sign reads, "Win your dream home." Leading up to the Fourth of July, dozens of stands line the highway filled with the illegal fireworks only Native Americans are allowed to sell. When I was a kid, my mom, my brother, and I would drive the 45 miles midweek to eat greasy vegetarian food (Yogi Burgers, Pronto Pups), shop for Heritage Singers records at the ABC, and purchase sticks of dynamite from the Muckleshoots.

People from all over our half of the state showed up on Sabbaths for camp meeting, bringing picnic lunches or arranging to meet up with friends who'd chosen to spend the week in a tent, caravan, or dormitory room. Everyone parked on the grass, and women walked gingerly to avoid getting their high heels stuck. Sometimes there'd be an offshoot group demonstrating on the highway with big ugly placards—"Adventists Kill Babies!" or "Come Out of Babylon!" We'd cringe with embarrassment, wondering what people thought. We'd wad up the badly printed leaflets stuck under our windshield wipers and throw them into the nearest bin. Later we'd discuss it over lunch: "Who are these Adventists who kill babies?" "Dunno. Must be in California."

When we were little, the staff in the children's departments would stamp our hands to say "green light" (meaning we were free to leave on our own).

When we were older, we'd loiter outside our designated meeting halls, flaunting our new dress or leather jacket, seeing and being seen, never quite making it inside.

When the meeting was over, we met our parents at the flagpole, in the center of the campus, and we'd have lunch—sometimes on our own at nearby Mud Mountain Dam—other times with "old friends" we couldn't escape, like one family who was made up of enormously fat people who brought a huge jar of pickles into which they simultaneously crammed all their pudgy hands, fishing in the green juice for the biggest prize, dripping pickle liquid all over the picnic blanket, wiping their soiled hands on their clothes, grinning with bits of food stuck in their teeth.

Of course there would always be the people who live self-sufficient-style in an Adventist commune and don't believe in deodorant or in wearing zippers in their clothes. You'd get the odd teenager, high on LSD he bought onto the reservation, screaming that his arms had turned into snakes. You'd have those grumpy old folks who refuse to smile. There were always screaming babies.

It was summer, so it was usually too hot, and you had to dress up, which made it seem hotter. It was unpleasant, but you had to accept invitations back to people's tents and drink cashew nut milk, otherwise they'd be offended. During the course of the week some kid would impale a frog on a stick and chase you with it. "Stay clear of those bathrooms," someone would warn. "Full of mites." These are my memories.

It was so bad it was good. It was a blast. Highlight of the year. You'd always bump into old friends you actually liked. Make a new best friend. There'd be an especially entertaining speaker. One year my mom was evening storyteller for the primary tent—and I was young enough to be proud instead of embarrassed.

One thing camp meeting was not was particularly *optional*. It's different in the U.K., where most people (at least where I lived) seemed barely aware there was a camp meeting. They attended their regular churches as usual. When I was growing up, they shut the churches down. They slapped a handwritten sign on the glass double doors: "Church closed. Go to Auburn Academy." Nobody argued with that. You didn't say, "I don't *do* camp meeting." You didn't complain about how it was too far/too tacky/too boring/too crowded. Well, maybe you complained—but you went anyway. Right along with everybody else. You were all hot and hungry and itchy together.

THE THING I'VE always loved about Thanksgiving in America, and missed terribly when I was in England, is that no matter where you are or who you are, you can pretty much guarantee that everyone is doing pretty much the same thing. Same sweet potatoes and pumpkin pie, same football game, same pigout-induced stupor. Shared experiences are what bring people together, what make us a community. It's the reason I can talk to just about any American on an airplane, and even if we're from different states or of different ages, ethnic groups, sexes, or economic groups, we will have a lot in common. In many ways we've lived the same life. Sharing experiences with people and being surrounded by those who understand you is not essential—ask anyone who's spent any significant time in a foreign country—but it's nice.

WHERE I'M FROM, in the Adventist world, if you're a local and you're roughly of my generation, you'll have probably attended Auburn Adventist Academy, and your photograph will hang on the walls of a long corridor along with pictures of your brothers and sisters, mom and dad, aunts and uncles, cousins, grandparents, great-aunts and great-uncles, and maybe even great-grandparents. You'll have gone to summer camp at Sunset Lake and been bucked off a horse and made to wash your own plates in dirty water and spent the night in a barn sneezing with your eyes swollen shut. You'll have been to Pathfinder Camporee during the winter, in a dirt storm, where you nearly died of hypothermia. If you're female, you ran the 100-meter dash in your Pathfinder pencil skirt and your dress shoes. You've been put "on social" for touching a member of the opposite sex. At least one grumpy old person at church will have told you you're going straight to hell. If you're a smart-mouth, you'll have answered, "Guess I'll see you there then." Popcorn and frozen fruit will have been your supper nearly every Saturday night of your life. You'll have attended Home and School movie nights at the local school where someone stands up and puts his hand over the projector to cover an on-screen kiss or any character smoking, and someone lowers the volume if there's a bad word.

If you're me, on your eighteenth birthday there was an Ellen G. White-themed day at church, and at the Ellen G. White-approved potluck (no butter or salt) all these people in nineteenth-century costume forced you to stand while they sang "Happy Birthday," and you thought, *This is so weird.*

Community is all those shared experiences—good and bad—that give you something to talk about. It is all those people—wonderful and annoying—who exist to save you from yourself, to keep an eye on you, to keep you pure, to tell your parents if they see you smoking or holding hands with a boy. When I was younger, I hated community—all those busybodies who wouldn't mind their own business. It seemed so restrictive. I couldn't move, couldn't breathe, couldn't wait to get out, to grow up, to leave and never come back. As you get older, of course, you realize that no one *has* to care about you at all. Community starts to look more attractive.

Part of growing up—and when I say growing up, I mean maturing, not merely aging—is accepting your community, warts and all. It's being able to say, "I wouldn't be the person I am today without the Muckleshoot Reservation and the costumed potluck." It's also recognizing that all those other things that you're tempted to think are "beneath" you as you become more sophisticated and travel farther away from where you began are really important and make up who you are.

THIS IS A hard truth to swallow, but not everything has to be to our liking. We need to repeat this at least once a day, or anytime we find ourselves forgetting that we are not, individually, the center of the universe. Remember, there is strength in numbers. There is beauty in accepting people as they are, even if they are different from you, or from the way you think a person ought to be.

When your life becomes about community and about experiences, you're less concerned with your own tastes. It gets easier to go with the flow, to enjoy a moment because you're in it—and alive, and not in physical pain—and you can find something worthwhile in that moment. Maybe you can share it with an old or new friend or a scowling geezer who doesn't like that you're wearing flip-flops. Community is about putting up (if that's the best you can do) with all sorts of people and believing that we are richer because of this mosaic of things that may not always make sense but that make our lives.

WHEN DINOSAURS
WALKED THE EARTH

THE WORD "NOSTALGIA" was coined in 1688 by a Swiss medical student. It is made up of two Greek roots and roughly means "The pain sick people feel because they wish to return to their native land and fear never to see it again." The word is commonly used, however, to refer to a longing for the past—a place none of us will ever see again. It's important, I think, to meditate on that fact a bit and really soak it in. We cannot return to the past. Ever.

I don't say this with glee. I'm no kind of past-hater. On the contrary, I think history—everything that has preceded us in our societies, families, churches, and communities—is extremely important in one way or another.

In fact, when I'm feeling overwhelmed with life, the thought that comforts me most is not the thought of a future heaven, but of the ancestors who came before me. Obviously I don't worship them, in the style of some cultures, but I think about the struggles they surmounted and allow myself to remember that the people who came before me have something to do with who I am. If they were strong, then so am I.

This doesn't mean that I can follow their examples perfectly. I'm not living their lives. I am not escaping persecution in France or giving birth in a cabin in northern Canada assisted by a drunken doctor. I have my own battles. What I can best draw from the past—personally—is the lesson that people are tough and resilient, that they can get through hard times.

What about our church history? There's a great deal of nostalgia for things like the "old" hymnal. This always makes me laugh, since the "new" hymnal came out when I was about 13. As far as I'm concerned, the new one is the old one. But that's not the case for a lot of people—many of whom also pine for things such as the "old" logo, which I don't recall seeing ever, not even once, until fairly recently on a Web site harking to get it back again.

The trouble with idealizing the past is that we tend to put our relics in pretty glass cases where the air can't break them down. And they sit there. And because they no longer work as effectively in the world as they used to—for whatever reason—they become nothing more than conversation pieces. Things to rant about.

What do you want? You want the church—its youth—to be the way young people used to be? Ain't gonna happen. People can't be the way people used to be. We don't even know what that means. We don't always know what it looks like. You ever watch old movies and marvel at how the people both talk and sing in a strange 1940s voice? Why do they talk that way? If you were magically transported back to 1942, you wouldn't fit in. We can't expect people to exist outside of their context. So what's plan B?

Maybe it's to look at people without using the yardstick of our past to measure them. Look at youth in your church and see them for what they are and for what they have to offer. Right now.

Recently I had a heated discussion in which I argued that—from what I see—youth today are improving. There is a level of awareness about a host of issues that simply didn't exist in my group during our teen years. These kids care about poverty and HIV/AIDS and environmental issues. They want to make the world a better place.

Anyway, as I was reminded last month on a trip to the Field Museum in Chicago—featuring dinosaurs and relics of Aztec ritualized killings (ripping the still-beating heart from the victim's chest)—the past wasn't all rosy. When I was about 12, for instance, my religious experience was focused almost solely on worrying about being executed in the electric chair for being a Sabbathkeeper. This was not, I fear, the best possible use of my time.

There are plenty of bad things about people, but one great quality is our ability to self-correct. We can see where we're out of focus and do something about it. And we can continue to draw strength from remembering that our church forebears were pioneers—and so are we.

A WARM PLACE
WITH NO MEMORY

"Do you think God lives in heaven because he too lives in fear of what he's cre-ated?—Spy Kids 2.

SOMEWHERE IN NORTHERN California a car breaks down. The oc-cupants—a mother and her 7-year-old daughter, Lucy—decide to have a milk shake at a nearby fast-food restaurant while waiting for roadside re-covery. As they take their seats near the window, a man named Kyle enters the restaurant. He is mentally ill and has a large deer-hunting rifle concealed beneath his long coat. Kyle was recently fired from his job at this very restau-rant. He is angry, but only wants to frighten the manager. The gun is un-loaded. When the police arrive, Kyle is waving his gun around, shouting. Kyle ignores a police order to drop his weapon, and a sniper—having Kyle lined up in his sights—squeezes his trigger. Just as he fires the gun, one of California's famous earthquakes rocks the town, knocking the sniper over. His shot goes a little wide, and the bullet hits little Lucy instead of Kyle, killing her instantly.

Who's to blame? Crazy Kyle? The authorities for failing to lock Kyle up? The manager for firing him? The police for being trigger-happy? The car manufacturer for faulty workmanship? The plate tectonics of the earth for such poor timing?

No one intended for Lucy to die. No one can argue there was any real evil or malice in this situation. And still, a little girl winds up dead. Even in the absence of anything we could rightly call evil, things in this world have a way of going pear-shaped. All the time. In California and in London. In Tehran and Sydney. In Nairobi and Buenos Aires.

What about God?

Why didn't He step in at some point: by keeping the car moving along; by striking Kyle down with a case of vomiting and diarrhea that would have kept him slumped over the toilet; by quieting the plate tectonics that rumble across the Pacific Rim? Everything that happens on this earth—good or bad—is God's responsibility, just as everything that happens on a home-owner's property is his or her responsibility. Check the steps of your walk-way. You can't hide from it: if someone breaks a leg, heads are gonna roll.

WHY DO INNOCENT people suffer? I can't think of a single answer I've ever heard that didn't make me roll my eyes. I can't think of one I'd feel comfortable spouting to Lucy's mother. "God allows you to suffer so He can reveal His glory through you." "With freedom comes suffering." "Everything will be made right in heaven." It isn't that I don't believe these arguments. There is truth in all of them, but truth can be a hollow thing when it's partial and incomplete and doesn't begin to abate your fears. When your insides turn to ice at receiving bad news, there's no *statement* that can make it better. It would be foolish to pretend otherwise, to offer a healing salve in a jar with simple instructions.

"If God is good," I asked someone recently, "why is the world bad?"

"The world isn't bad," the person said. "Not *all* bad. The world is *flawed.*"

"What's the difference?"

"Scale. Perspective. There's a lot of good in the world, in addition to the bad."

"Let me put it this way," I said. "What's the difference when your entire family has just been killed by a bus explosion in Egypt?"

"You got me," the person admitted.

But he's right. The world isn't *all* bad. Yet we're always asking *why.* Ultimately, it is a backward-looking question. It keeps you stuck. It doesn't let you breathe. Better to ask "How?" as in "Given that the world is as it is, *how* am I going to live?"

THE *SHAWSHANK REDEMPTION* tells the fictitious story of Andy Dufresne, falsely convicted of double murder and sentenced to life in a no-torious prison. He is routinely brutalized by a group of fellow prisoners and suffers every kind of loss you can imagine. The only thing he retains is hope. In the movie he says, "Hope is a good thing, maybe the best of things." After almost 20 years he escapes, crawling through a half mile of claustrophobic pipe crammed with raw sewage. Emerging at the end of the tube into a rainstorm, he lifts his head to the sky, raises his arms to the universe, and lets the water wash him clean. The past is over. Andy is starting fresh, on his way to "a warm place with no memory."

"I hate that movie," one of my friends said. "Unnecessarily violent."

Wrong. If Andy had crawled to freedom after almost 20 years spent sipping piña coladas by a pool in Puerto Vallarta, who would care? Because of his past, Andy savored freedom; he was happy. The scene makes you want to cheer.

Does God allow suffering so we can more fully appreciate the good things when they come our way? I'm afraid I couldn't say with any certainty. All I know for sure is this: there is good in the world, and I want to be part of that good. I want to hold on to hope. I cannot see that there is any real alternative. Bitterness? Anger? There's no redemption in those. God doesn't just give hope; God *is* hope. God *is* a "warm place with no memory."

While you're asking God "Why?" don't forget to toss out an occasional "Thank You" for everything good in your life. *People love me. I can run. I have sat under blossoming trees and read good books. I have felt the wind in my hair. I have lived.* If we're wise, we take the bad along with the good. We give thanks for what we have. We do the best we can for ourselves and for others. Above all, we *hope*.

All essays collected in this book were originally published in slightly different form as follows:

"Peace, Child" appeared in *Accent* magazine (General Conference Youth Department), 2008.

"Time on Your Hands" appeared in *The Rest of Your Life,* a book published by the South England Conference, 2006.

"Losing Your Donkey" appeared in the *Communicator,* South England Conference, 2006.

"Community" appeared in the *Communicator,* South England Conference, 2005.

"A Warm Place With No Memory" appeared in *Focus,* Stanborough Press, 2006.

All other essays were originally published in *HUB,* the youth journal of the South England Conference, between 2005 and 2008.